FROM CODFISH TO KIPPERS

Creative Recipes for Fresh, Smoked, and Salted Fish

ROGER PICKAVANCE

BOULDER
BOOKS

Library and Archives Canada Cataloguing in Publication

Title: From codfish to kippers : creative recipes for fresh, smoked, and salted fish / Roger
  Pickavance.
Names: Pickavance, Roger, 1943- author.
Description: Includes index.
Identifiers: Canadiana 20200321552 | ISBN 9781989417270 (softcover)
Subjects: LCSH: Cooking (Fish) | LCSH: Cooking, Canadian—Newfoundland and Labrador style. | LCGFT:
  Cookbooks.
Classification: LCC TX747 .P53 2020 | DDC 641.6/92—dc23

Design and layout: Todd Manning
Editor: Stephanie Porter
Copy editor: Iona Bulgin

Printed in Canada

We acknowledge the financial support of the Government
of Newfoundland and Labrador through the Department
of Tourism, Culture and Recreation.

Funded by the   Financé par le
Government   gouvernement   Canada
of Canada   du Canada

This book, like everything I write, is primarily for Priscilla, who loved food and drink, and seafood in particular. It is also for the rest of my extended Newfoundland family. As I remarked in my last book, their comments—opinionated, frequently caustic, but equally frequently complimentary—have been enormously helpful in my culinary development.

CONTENTS

INTRODUCTION

My previous book of recipes—*From Rum to Rhubarb*—was largely focused on food I learned to like or fully appreciate after coming to Newfoundland. This book necessarily takes a different tack, because fish in general are among the few things I have actively enjoyed for as long as I can remember.

One of my earliest childhood memories is going with my mother to the local fish shop, a white-tiled emporium, with fish displayed on a long, sloping slab covered with crushed ice. When I climbed out of the little pushchair that had conveyed me there, I had to stand on tiptoe to peer over the lower end of the slab. I remember admiring the red spots on a flatfish (a plaice I now realize) and reaching up and over the rim of the slab to feel the chill of the ice. I was listening to my mother asking the white-aproned fishmonger about how he got his fish in the inland town where we lived. I distinctly remember not understanding all the words in his answer, but equally clearly grasping the essence of it: the railway.

The Britain of my childhood had an extensive and complex rail network. The fishmonger explained that trawlers unloaded their catch in the evening in Grimsby on the English east coast—in those days the busiest fishing port in the world. The fish were whisked around the country overnight in railcars full of ice. One destination was Liverpool on the west coast. The fishmonger drove there very early every weekday morning to the big wholesale fish market, made his selections, and drove back with the fish in tubs of ice in the back of his van. The fish were on display on the slab by 9 a.m. This meant that the fish my mother was buying had still been on the boat a little over 12 hours previously.

Another early childhood memory was sitting in front of a small plate covered by a whole, cooked dab (a small flounder species), feeling content with the world as I prepared to eat the whole thing. And I remember fending off offers of help from my mother because I wanted the pleasure of picking it apart myself. I found almost all other foods put in front of me repugnant—I was the archetypal fussy eater—and later in life my mother assured me that fish had kept me alive through my childhood because it was one of the few foods she could tempt me to eat.

That fishmonger was the first of two sources of fish in my early life. The second was my father, a keen fly-fisherman, who regularly supplied our table with fresh trout—and the occasional grayling—throughout the season.

So I acquired my taste for fish at the beginning of my life and was therefore a natural fit for Newfoundland. But it proved paradoxical indeed that getting hold of fish here, even the ubiquitous cod, proved far more difficult than on the inland Welsh border.

THE RECIPES

To imply no favouritism, and for want of a better system, the featured fish are presented alphabetically, with a number of recipes under each. The instructions for each recipe are divided into two sections. First, there is a minimal description for the convenience of experienced cooks who need only general guidance. Following that are the *Notes*, where I have added explanatory detail for the benefit of the novice cook or those who are just curious about my modus operandi.

MEASUREMENTS

In *From Rum to Rhubarb* I explained in some detail the logic behind how I expressed weights and measures, which would be tedious to repeat here. A summary follows.

Bulk, dry ingredients such as sugar or flour, I specify weight in grams.

Bulk liquids such as milk or stock I specify in millilitres. However, I appreciate that many cooks will not have millilitre measures and would prefer to work in North American cups. They should hold in mind the following conversions, based on one North American cup approximately equalling 250 millilitres.

1 l = 1 qt	125 ml = ½ cup
250 ml = 1 cup	80 ml = ⅓ cup
190 ml = ¾ cup	65 ml = ¼ cup
170 ml = ⅔ cup	

But *small* quantities of dry (e.g., salt, ground spices) or liquid ingredients (e.g., vanilla essence, lemon juice), or herbs—chopped if fresh, crumbled if dry—are expressed in North American spoon measures for convenience and practicality. But if you think and measure in millilitres, bear the following approximations in mind.

1 tbsp = 15 ml	½ tsp = 2.5 ml
1 tsp = 5 ml	¼ tsp = 1.25 ml

In most of North America, temperatures of ovens and cooked foods are given in Fahrenheit, which I use here. All oven temperatures here refer to conventional ovens. If like me, you think in Celsius, the following approximate conversions will be helpful.

425°F = 220°C	275°F = 140°C
400°F = 200°C	250°F = 120°C
375°F = 190°C	225°F = 110°C
350°F = 180°C	220°F = 105°C
325°F = 165°C	200°F = 95°C
300°F = 150°C	175°F = 80°C

For all linear measurements I use the metric system. Here are approximate conversions for some commonly used utensil sizes and some frequently encountered chopping or slicing sizes.

28 cm = 11 in	3 cm = 1¼ in
25.5 cm = 10 in	6 mm = ¼ in
23 cm = 9 in	5 mm = ³⁄₁₆ in
20.5 cm = 8 in	3 mm = ⅛ in
5 cm = 2 in	2 mm = ³⁄₃₂ in

INGREDIENTS

Unless specified to the contrary, ingredients in the recipes are as follows.

Butter is standard commercial salted butter; unsalted can usually be substituted as long as you adjust the total salt in the recipe.

Cayenne is cayenne pepper, the ground spice, not the whole hot pepper.

Chèvre is cheese made from goat's milk; here the soft immature style is intended.

Coconut milk is a thick, oily extract of the white flesh of coconuts, not the watery fluid from inside the nut.

Cornstarch is finely ground corn (= maize), the same as corn flour in Britain. Not the same as the coarser cornmeal (= maize meal).

Cream is standard North American whipping cream at about 35% milk fat.

Dijon mustard is prepared French (or in that style) mustard; milder than English mustard.

Eggs are standard Canadian large; around 60 g per egg.

Flour is Canadian all-purpose, unbleached white (with about 13% protein).

Ghee is clarified butter cooked until it has a nutty aroma; how to make it is explained in the text.

Herbs are either finely chopped fresh, or dry and crumbled, measured by volume.

Milk is standard Canadian pasteurized, full-fat, whole milk at about 3.25% milk fat (although 1% or 2% milk can be substituted in most recipes).

Pepper is black pepper, freshly ground.

Prepared horseradish is the ready-to-use commercial, coarse paste of horseradish, not the freshly grated root.

Saffron is the best quality Spanish or Iranian saffron, in threads, not powder.

Salt is finely granulated, iodized table salt.

Shallots are small, pungent, brown-skinned, often bilobed members of the onion family. Some places use the name for what are usually called green onions (= spring onions).

Sour cream is artificially soured, commercial sour cream.

Spices are dry, ground; specified by volume.

Worcestershire sauce is a proprietary brand of savoury, vinegar sauce, based on anchovies and tamarind. The original brand is Lea and Perrins, still the best and the one by which others are judged.

SOURCES OF RECIPES

I frequently remember where and when I first ate some particular dish that inspired me, but I am rarely able to quote the provenance of my recipes because there is usually no single source. I read and talk eclectically about food, and then all those multiple influences go into the melting pot when I get around to cooking my own version of something.

THE COURSES OF A MEAL

I will sometimes use the terms amuse, appetizer, or main when talking about how many a particular recipe will serve.

Amuse is short for *amuse-bouche*—mouth-pleaser in French. These are typically single-bite-sized portions of something particularly flavourful. In restaurants, these are customarily served at the table and are often how a chef shows off a signature technique or ingredient. But domestically, they are better passed around while milling about with pre-dinner drinks.

Some people dismiss these as mere fripperies, but I see them as essential accompaniments to the necessary drink before dinner, a little something tasty to both whet the appetite and complement whatever you are drinking.

The appetizer is the small course, usually served at the table, which precedes the main course. Do not confuse this with the amuse.

As you would expect, the main course (at lunch or dinner) is exactly that, with dessert as the final course—but that is not the concern of this book.

COD, FRESH and SMOKED

Gadus morhua

FRESH COD

Cod Biryani

Cod Pie

Cod au Gratin

Cod Hot Pot

SMOKED COD

Smoked Cod Chowder

Smoked Cod Custards

Smoked Cod Lasagne

Although fresh, smoked, and salt cod are all the same species of fish, I have separated salt cod into its own chapter because it behaves like a completely different fish: different taste, different texture, different cooking methods.

Cod created the Newfoundland we know today. Europeans initially came here seasonally to catch cod. Then they took to living here year-round, which created the pattern of settlement and traditional way of life that characterized this island for so long. Salt cod was the primary commercial product of the fisherman or fishing family—simply because it would keep in pre-refrigeration days—but fresh cod has always been enjoyed domestically at the same time, although my recipes below are certainly not traditional.

FRESH COD

*B*iryani (or *biriani*) is a word of Persian origin referring to a style of cooking that came to India with the Mogul invaders. The word originally simply meant *fried*, but now loosely means any dish of flavoured—particularly with saffron—and spiced rice layered or mixed with meat, fish, or vegetables.

I am always in fear of the wrath of purists, so had originally thought to call this dish "Cod with Onions and Spiced Rice." But since there are countless regional variations under the general rubric of biryani, encompassing a bewildering variety of preparations, I feel fairly safe in adopting the same name for my recipe.

COD BIRYANI

serves 4 as a main course

500 g cod, trimmed weight

Rice
200 g long-grain rice
375 ml stock (fish, chicken, or vegetable)
1¾ tsp salt
2 pinches saffron

Spiced onions
750 g onion, trimmed weight
2 garlic cloves
30 g fresh ginger, trimmed weight
3 tbsp oil
1 tsp cumin
¼ tsp cayenne

Garnish
30 g slivered almonds
6 tomatoes, grape size
  or garnish of your choice

Preheat the oven to 350°F. Wash and soak the rice. Chop the onion coarsely or finely. Sliver garlic and ginger. Cut the cod into about 20 pieces (about 25 g each). Toast the almonds in the oven.

Bring the stock to a simmer with the salt and saffron. Turn off the heat and let infuse for at least 30 minutes or until ready to use.

Drain the soaked rice, add to the saucepan of stock, bring back to a boil, and simmer 2 to 3 minutes until the surface is pocked. Turn down the heat as low as possible, cook for 15 minutes, then turn off the heat and leave until ready to use.

Fry the onion, ginger, and garlic on medium-high heat until soft, translucent, and browned in places. Add the cumin and cayenne and cook another minute.

Cod Biryani

Mix the cooked rice with the onion-spice mixture and spread about one-third of it inside a baking dish. Evenly space the chunks of cod on the layer of rice, then spread the rest of the rice mixture over the top, poking it down to fill crevices, and then smoothing the top. Cover with a lid or foil and bake about 30 minutes.

Remove the lid or foil, sprinkle on the toasted almonds and sliced tomatoes, and serve at once.

NOTES

Use a good-quality basmati or other long-grain rice; do not use a short-grain rice.

Washing and soaking the rice is an important step. Dry rice is dusty with powdered starch, which needs to be washed off. Then the rice needs soaking to ensure even cooking.

Many recipes say wash the rice until the washing water runs clear, but this is misleading because no matter how many times you change the water, it will always be slightly cloudy. Usually three or four changes will suffice, as long as you agitate the rice as you rinse it.

The soaking time depends on the temperature of the water and the dryness of the rice. Typically it takes about an hour, but be guided by the colour: when all the grains have turned an opaque, chalky white, it's soaked enough.

Saffron is notoriously expensive because it consists of stigmas of the saffron crocus laboriously picked by hand and then dried (the species has three stigmas per flower, so it's not *quite* as tedious as it sounds). It is also notoriously difficult to quantify, so most recipes specify pinches—but what is a pinch? As a guide, my pinches are about 25 individual threads of saffron, so the above recipe has about 50 threads. To calibrate *your* pinch, take a few pinches from your jar of saffron and count the threads. This is easiest if you have high-quality saffron with a majority of unbroken threads, but inevitably not all threads will be intact, so assemble them as necessary from fragments.

Chop the onion according to whether you like large chunks of (cooked) onion in your food, or small pieces that melt into the background. But sliver or mince the garlic and ginger finely so that numerous small pieces are dispersed throughout the dish.

Toast the almonds in the oven, turning over at least once, about 7 to 8 minutes or until nicely browned. Be careful toward the end of the cooking time: they go from undercooked to burnt very rapidly.

A useful size of baking dish is about 20 by 20 centimetres, or the equivalent in an oval or rectangular dish.

The next three recipes are variations on the same theme, but all have different characteristics and are among my favourite ways of enjoying fresh cod. I distinguish them as follows: the pie has mashed potato on top, hot pot is covered with sliced potato, and cod au gratin has a topping of bread crumbs and cheese with no potato at all. These are personal distinctions which are certainly not recognized by all cooks.

When pie is mentioned one assumes pastry, but not all pies are covered in pastry—think shepherd's pie with its layer of mashed potato, just like my cod pie. The ingredient list looks dauntingly long, but the recipe is quite straightforward because the process is divided into well-defined stages.

COD PIE

serves 4 as a main course

400 g fresh cod
75 g small shrimp
125 g smoked cod, trimmed weight

For the mashed potatoes
500 g potatoes, trimmed weight
50 g butter
2 tbsp cream
1 tbsp prepared horseradish

For the poaching liquid
50 g shallot, trimmed weight
1 garlic clove
250 ml fish (or chicken) stock
65 ml dry white wine
1 allspice berry
1 bay leaf
milk as needed

For the sauce
50 g butter
50 g shallot, trimmed weight
3 tbsp flour
65 ml cream
¼ tsp salt
¹⁄₁₆ tsp cayenne
15 g parsley (optional)

To brush on top
25 g butter

If your smoked cod and shrimp are frozen, thaw them ahead of time. Peel the potatoes and cut into chunks. Thinly slice the garlic and 50 grams of shallot. Finely chop the other 50-gram portion of shallot.

Put the stock, sliced shallot, garlic, wine, allspice, and bay leaf in a small saucepan and bring to a boil, then simmer about 30 minutes. Then slide in the smoked fish (but not the fresh fish), cut to fit the saucepan if necessary. Immediately turn off the heat, cover the saucepan, and leave for 10 minutes. Remove the fish, brushing off any solids clinging to it, and slice or coarsely flake the fish; reserve.

Strain the poaching liquid, press on the solids caught in the sieve to extract as much juice as possible, and discard the solids. Measure the strained juice and make up to 250 millilitres with milk. Reserve.

Boil the chunked potatoes in salted water until tender. Drain, then dry off on a low heat. Mash with 50 grams of butter, the cream, and horseradish. Reserve, but keep warm.

Melt the other 50 grams of butter in a medium saucepan over a low heat, add the finely chopped shallot, and cook on a low heat for about 5 minutes, or until soft and translucent. Then stir in the flour and cayenne, and cook another 5 minutes. Whisk in the reserved stock, cream, and salt. Heat and whisk continuously until it thickens, then simmer for about 10 minutes.

Preheat the oven to 350°F. Melt the 25 grams of butter. Drain the shrimp of any excess fluid.

Cut the fresh cod into large chunks. Take the sauce off the heat, stir in the parsley if using. Mix in the sliced or flaked smoked fish, cubed fresh fish, and shrimp. Transfer this mixture to a baking pan that will hold the cod chunks in a single layer and smooth the surface. Spread the mashed potatoes over the top. Furrow the top with a fork, brush with melted butter, and put in the oven.

Bake about 30 minutes or until the top is lightly golden. Turn on the broiler, if necessary, for the last few minutes to get the top appetizingly brown.

NOTES

If you are making this for someone with a shellfish allergy, simply substitute an extra 75 grams of cod or smoked cod for the shrimp.

If possible, buy loins of cod, which are approximately the same thickness along their length, making it easier to cut into same-size chunks. A chunk to me is about 20 to 25 grams, so that 400 grams of cod will cut into about 16 to 20 pieces. If you can only get full fillets—a loin plus a thinner tail piece—cut the tail part into pieces which when folded over will approximate the bigger chunks from the loin.

The common, small shrimp (*Pandalus borealis*) of the northwest Atlantic are ideal for this dish, and they are widely available in Newfoundland—at least in the frozen state. They are wild-caught and much better flavoured than most farmed shrimp.

A 20 by 20-centimetre pan, or equivalent in a different shape, will hold the cod in one layer.

Use a high- or medium-starch variety of potato that is good for mashing. I use russets. If you use a lower-starch potato, you will get less fluffy mash, which you may in fact prefer. To get the required 500 grams trimmed weight, start with about 800 grams of whole, unpeeled potatoes. If not cooking them immediately after cutting into chunks, reserve them covered in cold water to prevent discolouration. Chunks of potato will typically take about 15 to 20 minutes to cook in salted water, which is 1 teaspoon of salt per litre of water.

Keeping the mashed potato warm makes it easier to spread. If you find it tricky to spread the mashed potato over the fish mixture, try laying multiple small blobs of mashed potato over the top of the mixture, then gently nudge them together before furrowing the surface with a fork.

Time under the broiler is difficult to specify because broilers vary so much, but 5 minutes would be typical.

Cod *au gratin* is immensely popular in Newfoundland—deservedly so—to the point where many people think of it as a traditional food. The name has certainly become thoroughly naturalized, usually pronounced as all one word, something like *codergrattun*.

It is derived from the French *au gratin* dishes, where some savoury food is sprinkled with bread crumbs or cheese or both, and browned in a hot oven or under a broiler. For me it's that cheese and bread-crumb topping that distinguishes it from other baked cod dishes, and it's one of the few occasions where I like fish with cheese.

COD AU GRATIN

serves 4 as a main course

500 g cod, trimmed weight
100 g shallot
50 g butter
2 tbsp white wine
1 tsp dry vermouth
5 tbsp flour
375 ml milk
1 tsp Dijon mustard
½ tsp Worcestershire sauce
1 tsp salt
¼ tsp pepper
¼ tsp nutmeg

For topping
50 g old, crumbly cheddar
40 g bread crumbs, dry
15 g butter to pre-toast the crumbs,
 optional

Finely chop the shallot. Cut the cod into pieces, about 20 to 25 grams each. Grate the cheese. Preheat the oven to 375°F.

Sweat the shallot in the butter until soft and translucent but not browned. Add the wine and vermouth and reduce to a glaze.

Whisk in the flour, whisk in the milk, and whisk until thickened into a béchamel sauce. Add the mustard, Worcestershire sauce, salt, pepper, and nutmeg.

When ready to bake, mix the sauce with the cubed fish, then spread it evenly over the base of a 20 by 20-centimetre baking dish, smoothing the top.

Mix the grated cheese with the crumbs and spread evenly over the top of the dish.

Bake about 30 minutes. For a darker brown top, use pre-toasted crumbs and/or turn on the broiler for the last 5 minutes.

NOTES

See the comments under Cod Pie about cutting cod into chunks. For notes on making béchamel, see Cod Hot Pot.

For this dish, be very conservative when adding flavourings to the sauce because the fish has to be the primary taste. Similarly, do not add herbs such as tarragon or savoury to the topping for fear of overwhelming the fish.

Most strongly flavoured, meltable cheeses will work in this recipe. The traditional cheeses in French *au gratin* dishes are Emmenthal, Comté, or Beaufort. Swiss Gruyère is also often used, but a good sharp, crumbly cheddar—but not a rubbery, mild one—works very well.

In a 375°F oven, the top will lightly brown in 30 minutes. If a darker brown top is preferred, pre-brown the crumbs: melt about 15 grams of butter in a frying pan and toss and stir the crumbs around in it until golden brown. Let cool before mixing with the cheese. Alternatively (or as well) turn on the broiler for the last few minutes of cooking. See the notes about broiling times under Cod Pie.

My cod hot pot takes its inspiration from dishes from the north of England like Lancashire hot pot, a casserole of meat and onions covered with layers of sliced potato. It is no relation to East Asian hot pots, where small pieces of food are cooked in simmering broth at the table.

COD HOT POT

serves 4 as a main course

500 g cod, trimmed weight
150 g small shrimp

For the leek sauce
100 g leeks, trimmed weight
4 garlic cloves
50 g butter
60 ml white wine
2 tbsp flour
250 ml milk
1 tsp Dijon mustard
1 tsp prepared horseradish
½ tsp salt
¼ tsp pepper

The potato topping
650 g potatoes, trimmed weight
30 g butter
salt and pepper

If your shrimp are frozen, thaw them ahead of time and drain off any accumulated fluid before using them. Chop the leek; finely chop the garlic. Cut the cod into same-size chunks. Preheat the oven to 350°F. Cut the peeled potatoes into same-size chunks and poach them in salted water until barely cooked.

Sweat the leeks and garlic in a saucepan in the 50 grams of butter until soft but not browned. Add the wine and reduce to a glaze. Whisk in the flour, then whisk in the milk to make a béchamel sauce. Whisk in the mustard, horseradish, salt, and pepper. Cover and reserve.

When ready to bake, mix the chunks of cod and the shrimp with the béchamel and spread this evenly in a dish that will hold the cod chunks in one layer.

Slice the cooked potatoes thickly. Layer the slices on top of the sauce-fish mixture, cutting pieces as necessary to make two snugly fitting layers. Melt the 25 grams of butter, brush over the top of the potatoes, and sprinkle with salt and pepper to taste.

Bake about 30 to 35 minutes. Turn on the broiler for the last few minutes to brown the top.

NOTES

If you are making this for someone with a shellfish allergy, simply replace the shrimp with an extra 75 grams of cod.

The easiest way to chop the leek is to cut the trimmed leek lengthways into four or six strips, then slice thinly crossways.

I use Yukon Gold potatoes for this dish. To get the required 650 grams of trimmed potatoes, start with about 1 kilogram of unpeeled potatoes. The potatoes *must* be pre-cooked because the fish would become badly over-cooked in the time raw potatoes on top would need. But do not pre-cook potatoes to the point of falling apart—12 to 15 minutes is typically long enough, depending on size. Slice the cooked potatoes about 5 millimetres thick.

To make a béchamel (white sauce): melt the butter in a small saucepan on a medium heat. Whisk in the flour until completely homogeneous. Turn down the heat and let the flour cook in the butter for 2 minutes. Pour in all the milk at once, turn up the heat, and whisk until a thick sauce forms. Turn down the heat, add the flavourings, and simmer about another 5 minutes, whisking frequently.

A useful size of baking dish which will hold the chunks of fish in one layer is about 20 by 20 centimetres, or use any shaped dish of equivalent size.

The notes in the previous recipe about the shrimp, cutting up the cod, and the time under the broiler also apply here.

SMOKED COD

Some readers may recognize this chowder as a riff on *Cullen Skink*, a speciality of the northeast coast of Scotland, where the eponymous little town of Cullen is located. But I am not calling it that for fear of purists' wrath. In addition, I have always been slightly put off by the *skink* part of the name, which derives from the old Scots dialect word meaning shin of beef, hence the soup made from that, and then transposed to a fish soup. Despite the name, the soup is excellent, and although smoked haddock was traditional—and no doubt insisted upon by purists—I think our local smoked cod is superior to the smoked haddock we can buy here, if it can be found at all.

For me the combination of leeks and fish is particularly felicitous, although onion or shallots can be used if that's what you have.

SMOKED COD CHOWDER

serves 4 as a lunch main course

150 g leeks, trimmed weight
25 g butter
1 whole clove
1 bay leaf
250 ml chicken stock
450 g potatoes, trimmed weight
500 ml milk, plus extra to thin
250 g smoked cod, trimmed weight
1/16 tsp cayenne
1/8 tsp pepper
1/4 tsp salt, or to taste

For the garnish
chives or parsley, optional

Chop the leeks finely. Trim the potatoes and cut into 1-centimetre cubes. Sliver the trimmed, raw, smoked cod thinly. Chop some chives or parsley for garnish.

Sweat the slivered leeks in a saucepan in the butter until soft and completely cooked but not browned.

Add the cubed potatoes, clove, bay leaf, and chicken stock to the saucepan. Bring to a boil, then simmer until the potatoes are just tender. Remove the clove and bay leaf. Remove about 250 millilitres of the potato cubes, plus whatever leeks come with them, and put in a small jug that will fit the end of your hand blender. Add enough of the milk so that the potatoes blend to a smooth cream.

Return this to the saucepan, with the rest of the milk, cayenne, black pepper, salt, and the slivered cod. Bring slowly to a simmer. Do not let it boil; just bring the milk to a scald and the fish will be cooked.

Serve at once, in warmed soup bowls; sprinkle with chopped chives or parsley if liked.

NOTES

Try not to use floury potatoes for this dish, as there is a risk they will fall apart; I use Yukon Gold. To get 450 grams of trimmed potatoes, start with about 700 grams of unpeeled potatoes. Small cubes of potato will take about 10 to 15 minutes to cook.

For tips on chopping leeks, see Cod Hot Pot.

The exact thickness of this soup is controlled by the amount (if any) of the extra milk that is added.

Smoked Cod Chowder

SMOKED COD CUSTARDS

makes 6 appetizer portions

300 g smoked cod, trimmed weight
4 eggs
250 ml cream
¼ tsp pepper
1 tsp Dijon mustard
2 tbsp chives

Preheat the oven to 350°F. Wrap the smoked cod in foil. Finely mince the chives and measure out. Boil a kettle of water.

Bake the foil packet of smoked cod about 12 to 15 minutes. When cool enough to handle, flake coarsely, and reserve. Also reserve any juices from the packet.

Whisk together the eggs, pepper, mustard, and cream. Stir in the minced chives, flaked cod, and any reserved juices.

Divide this between 6 ramekins. Bake these in a *bain-marie* for about 30 to 35 minutes or until just set.

Serve warm with crusty bread.

NOTES

For this recipe I use standard 150-millilitre ramekins, each about 7.5 centimetres diameter by 3.5 centimetres deep internally.

Note that there is no added salt in this recipe—the smoked fish is usually salty enough by itself.

A *bain-marie* is essentially a water bath in the oven. Find a shallow baking dish that holds the ramekins comfortably with some space between them, and put in the filled ramekins. Put the baking dish half-in and half-out of the oven—slightly more in than out for safety. Bring the kettle of water back to a full boil, and carefully pour in boiling water to come about halfway up the ramekins. Be *very* careful not to splash any water into the ramekins. If space is tight, remove one of the ramekins, pour the boiling water into that space, then replace the ramekin just before you push the baking dish fully into the oven. Push cautiously to avoid making waves in the baking tray which might flood the ramekins. Rotate the baking tray about halfway through the cooking time.

Judging when the custards are cooked is tricky. When you nudge the edge of the pan, the custards should not slosh in their middles, but merely wobble. Try to avoid cooking them until they are set solidly firm.

SMOKED COD LASAGNE

serves 6 as a main course

For poaching the smoked cod
500 g smoked cod, trimmed weight
750 ml milk
1 onion
1 whole clove
1 bay leaf

Noodles
12 pieces dry lasagne noodle
butter to grease a baking dish

Béchamel sauce
625 ml of the milk used for poaching,
  plus extra if needed
50 g butter
5 tbsp flour
½ tsp salt
1 tbsp Dijon mustard

Cheese and spinach
142 g baby spinach
50 g old, crumbly cheddar

Topping
190 ml béchamel
  (taken from the main batch)
1 egg
¼ of the 50 g of the cheddar

Preheat the oven to 350°F. Lightly grease a baking dish that will hold 3 cooked noodles in one layer. Peel the onion but otherwise leave it whole.

Smoked cod
Stick the clove into the peeled onion. Put this with the bay leaf and the 750 millilitres of milk in a small saucepan and bring to a simmer. Turn off the heat and leave to infuse with the lid on for about 30 minutes. Then bring back to a simmer, add the smoked cod, turn off the heat again, and let stand for about 10 minutes or until the cod flakes easily when prodded with a fork.

Lift out the cooked cod, and when cool enough to handle, flake coarsely, and reserve. Strain off the solids from the milk, pressing down firmly on them in the sieve to extract as much fluid as possible. Discard the solids; reserve the strained milk.

Noodles
Bring a large, wide pot of salted water to a boil and poach the noodles until barely tender—typically around 9 minutes, or according to manufacturer's instructions. Plunge them into cold water to wait upon final assembly.

Cheese and spinach
Grate the cheese coarsely and divide into four portions.

Cook the spinach briefly in boiling, salted water until completely wilted, strain and dry it, then chop it finely.

Béchamel sauce
Measure the reserved, strained, cod-poaching milk; make it up to 625 millilitres with extra milk if necessary.

Melt the butter in a saucepan, and make a béchamel sauce with the milk, salt, and mustard. Remove and reserve about 190 millilitres of the béchamel for the topping.

Stir the cooked, chopped spinach, the cooked, flaked smoked cod, and three-quarters of the cheese into the remaining approximately 435 millilitres of béchamel, then divide this into three portions.

The topping
Whisk the egg and one-quarter of the grated cheese into the 190 millilitres of reserved béchamel.

To assemble
Top layer: 190 ml béchamel sauce, mixed with the egg and ¼ of the grated cheese
layer 7: 3 cooked noodles, trimmed to fit
layer 6: ⅓ spinach-cod-cheese sauce
layer 5: 3 cooked noodles, trimmed to fit
layer 4: ⅓ spinach-cod-cheese sauce
layer 3: 3 cooked noodles, trimmed to fit
layer 2: ⅓ spinach-cod-cheese sauce
bottom layer: 3 cooked noodles, trimmed to fit, on top of butter smeared on the bottom of the dish

Bake about 75 to 90 minutes or until the top is nicely browned.

NOTES

The lasagne noodle I use is about 5 by 25 centimetres dry size.

For this recipe I use a Pyrex glass baking dish, about 18 by 28 centimetres; this will accommodate 3 cooked noodles with ends trimmed to make them fit exactly.

Generously salt the water to cook the noodles: at least 1 teaspoon of salt per litre of water.

Cooked spinach usually needs drying before using. The first step is to let it drain in a sieve and press down on it to get rid of the bulk of the water. Then gather it into one mass and squeeze it as firmly as you can between your hands until it's difficult to get any more water to dribble out of it. Then roll it tightly in a kitchen towel and twist the ends of the towel in opposite directions to squeeze out the last drop of water, which will soak into the towel.

For notes on making béchamel sauce, see Cod Hot Pot.

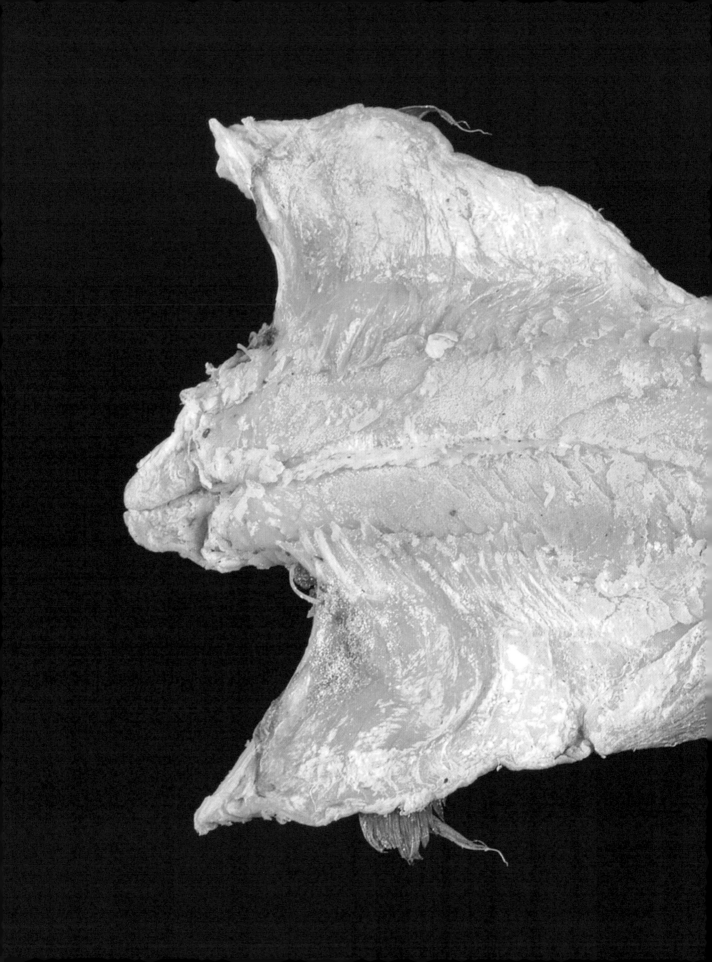

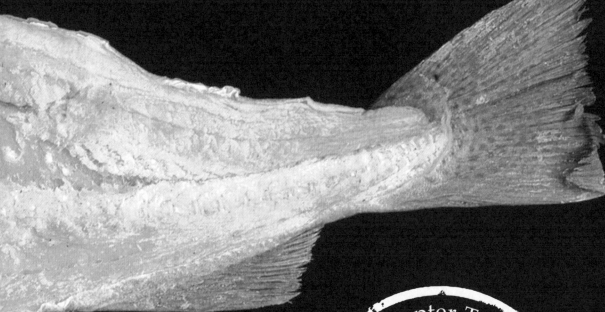

Chapter Two

SALT COD

SALT COD

Salt Cod, Potato, and Onion Casserole

Salt Cod Brandade

Eggs Benedictine

Brandade Fish Cakes

Salt Cod in Béchamel Sauce

Salt Cod Frittata

Salt Cod and Chickpea Salad

Salt Cod and Potato Salad

Salt Cod and Avocado Salad

n her excellent book *The Hungry Empire*, Lizzie Collingham points out that the industrial-scale production of salt cod on Newfoundland's shores, in full swing by the 17th century, was the first step in what became Britain's global trading empire. That salt cod business—and other enterprises—needed both a merchant marine to transport the goods and a fighting force, the Royal navy, to protect production and transport. So the whole world should thank, or blame, Newfoundland for all that.

Salt cod is still made in Newfoundland, mostly for domestic use. But at its height, the Newfoundland salt cod trade exported massive quantities to much of central Europe, Britain, the Mediterranean nations, the Caribbean, and parts of South America.

Most of the Mediterranean nations where salt cod has long been an important part of the cuisine have a similar name for it, probably all derived from the Basque name *bakailao*. This is not surprising because it was the Basques who were among the first to commercially exploit the idea of salting and drying the cod they caught on the banks of Newfoundland. The name was adopted by the Portuguese (*bacalhau*), the Spanish (*bacalao*), the Catalans (*bacallà*), the Italians (*baccalà*), and the Greeks (*bakaliaros*).

The French, however, are an exception to this; they have their *morue salée*—or often simply *morue*. I think this reflects the fact that they, alongside the Basques, were one of the original exploiters of Newfoundland cod, so coined their own name, rather than simply following the Basque nomenclature.

INTRODUCTORY NOTES ON SALT COD

Salt cod dishes are covered in many published works, in particular Edward Jones's *Salt Cod Cuisine*, a mine of information, and I have chosen my recipes to avoid too much duplication of that excellent book.

My salt cod recipes usually start with a specified weight of cooked, trimmed-weight salt cod, so the necessary preliminaries can conveniently be dealt with here. These consist of three stages: soaking, poaching, and trimming.

Soaking the dry salt cod is essential to get rid of most of the salt. Ways of doing this vary. I have met people in rural parts of Newfoundland who peg a whole salt cod down in a small freshwater stream and leave it there for a day. But more usually salt cod—cut up if necessary—is left in a bowl of fresh water for 24 or more hours, changing the water every 4 to 6 hours.

Knowing how long to soak is tricky, because unless you are very experienced you will usually have no idea how much salt is in the piece of salt cod in front of you. Some people claim to be able to judge by chewing a small fragment, or even licking the salt cod. Maybe, but I am dubious.

I always soak salt cod for at least 24 hours with several changes of water. If it's a really thick piece of salt cod (more than about 5 centimetres at thickest point), I soak it for 48 hours. But if in any doubt, I simply soak for the longer time—salt can always be added to the finished dish if necessary, and remember that any excess saltiness will be offset by the lack of salt in other ingredients.

Poach the soaked salt cod in a wide and shallow saucepan. I routinely use a pan about 30 centimetres diameter, about 5 or 6 litres capacity, if necessary cutting the salt cod in pieces to fit.

Bring about 4 litres of water to a boil in the pan you have chosen with 1 small, whole, peeled onion, 2 bay leaves, and 2 cloves. Put the lid on the pan, turn off the heat, and leave to infuse at least 30 minutes or until you need to cook the salt cod.

When ready to cook the soaked salt cod, bring the water back to a full rolling boil, slide in the fish (or pieces of fish), immediately turn off the heat, cover the pan, and leave to cook for 15 minutes—or 20 minutes if it's a thicker piece (greater than 5 centimetres).

Remove the poached salt cod from the water, drain, and leave until cool enough to handle. Then remove all skin and bones, using a small paring knife and your fingers.

Although most recipes say discard the skin along with the bones, I like to retain most of the skin from the fish and incorporate it into the finished dish. It imparts a slightly gelatinous quality, which some people claim not to like, and they often object to the speckled appearance it also imparts. Your choice, but if you've never tried it, do so.

The yield of cooked fish varies according to which part of the whole salt cod you are dealing with. Thicker parts, toward the head end, will typically yield 75 to 80 per cent of the dry, salted weight in cooked, edible fish. Thinner parts, toward the tail, will yield 50 to 65 per cent of the dry, salted weight.

But when buying salt cod, I avoid any on-the-spot mental arithmetic, and simply assume a minimum 50 per cent yield; that is, I buy twice as much salt cod, dry, on-the-bone weight as I will need for my recipe. This always creates a small surplus of cooked fish—an excuse to make a small batch of *brandade* or a little salt cod frittata for myself.

Although I do admit the convenience of boneless salt cod fillets, I always prefer salt cod cooked on the bone because I think it has a better taste and texture. For me, the minimal extra effort of taking the cooked fish off the bone is well worth it. And salt cod on the bone is as easily kept as fillet: split a whole salt cod in half lengthways, use what you need, freeze any surplus.

Some readers will recognize this dish as a version of the classic Portuguese *Bacalhau à Gomes de Sá*, but I don't use that name here because—unlike, say, *brandade*—it is not well established in English-speaking culinary circles.

SALT COD, POTATO, and ONION CASSEROLE

serves 4 as a main course

500 g salt cod, cooked, trimmed weight

The onions and potatoes
500 g onions, trimmed weight
3 garlic cloves
65 ml olive oil, plus more to brush
1 kg potatoes, trimmed weight
4 tbsp olive oil
pepper to taste
salt as needed

Garnish
4 eggs
12 black olives
parsley

Hard boil the eggs, and just before serving slice them thickly or cut into wedges. Cut the olives in half lengthways after removing the pits. Chop the parsley finely. Slice the onions into semi-circles about 5 millimetres thick. Thinly slice the garlic. Soak, cook, and trim the salt cod as per the Introductory Notes. Reserve the cooked fish and the poaching water separately. Preheat the oven to 350°F.

Add salt to the poaching water, and poach the whole, peeled potatoes in this until just tender (30 to 40 minutes according to size). Alternatively, discard the fish-poaching water, and boil the potatoes in new, salted water. Slice the potatoes thickly—about 1 centimetre—and reserve.

Fry the sliced onion in 65 millilitres of oil until browning at the edges. Add the sliced garlic for the last minute. Cover and reserve.

Brush a baking dish with oil. To check the saltiness, taste a small portion of fish with a bit of potato, and add more salt if needed as you assemble the dish.

Layer the components in the oiled baking dish as follows. Break the potato slices into smaller pieces as necessary to make a close-fitting layer.

1/2 the potatoes on top
1/2 the fish
1/2 the onion
1/2 the fish
1/2 the onion
1/2 the potatoes on bottom

Sprinkle each layer lightly with salt and pepper as needed.

Pour the remaining 4 tablespoons of oil evenly over the top layer of potatoes, and bake uncovered for about 30 to 40 minutes—or longer if the components were cold when assembled.

Turn on the broiler for the last few minutes to brown the top before serving. To serve, sprinkle with chopped parsley, and arrange the wedges or slices of hard-boiled egg and the half-olives on top.

NOTES

If you do not have your own particular way of hard-boiling eggs, here is what I do. Put the eggs, straight from the fridge, in a small saucepan and just cover with cold water. Bring to a full boil on a high heat, then turn down the heat, put the lid on the saucepan, and simmer them for 10 minutes. Then immediately transfer them to a bowl of cold water and leave until ready to peel.

There are dozens of different ways of frying onions. Here, I fry the sliced onions in oil on maximum heat, stirring and turning them over continually—a sort of stir-frying—until they are starting to soften, and browning at the edges with occasional dark scorched bits (about 6 to 8 minutes). Then I cover the pan, turn off the heat and let stand until needed. They don't have to be completely soft at this stage because they will soften further as they sit in the covered pan.

For this recipe I frequently use an oval baking dish, about 23 by 30 centimetres, but any oven-proof dish of similar size will serve.

The top should be nicely browned when the dish is served, which usually means turning on the broiler. You will need to judge by the browning how long the dish should be broiled.

The garnishes are important to the overall success of this dish. In particular I recommend you do not use ready-pitted olives, which have a far inferior flavour to those you pit yourself.

The word *brandade,* although allowed (in italics) by most of the authoritative English language dictionaries, is creeping only slowly into common English usage. The Oxford Dictionary definition is "a Provençal dish made from salt cod," but the meaning in culinary circles is far more specific: a purée of salt cod with olive oil, cream, garlic, and often potato.

Many of the salt cod-eating nations have some version of this dish, like the Italian *Baccalà mantecato,* a whipped purée of salt cod, but most cooks of the English-speaking world use the French word *brandade.*

SALT COD BRANDADE

makes 4 to 6 appetizer portions, or about 60 to 70 amuse portions

250 g salt cod, cooked, trimmed weight
85 ml olive oil plus extra if liked/needed
85 ml cream or milk, plus extra
  if liked/needed
125 g potatoes, cooked, trimmed weight
2 garlic cloves
½ tsp pepper
salt as needed, to taste

Accompaniments to serve
lemon wedges
pepper
crisp toasts (recipe below)

Soak, poach, and trim the salt cod as per the Introductory Notes. Reserve the poaching water.

Boil the peeled potatoes in the poaching water until tender. Alternatively, discard the fish-poaching water, and boil unpeeled potatoes in salted water. If necessary, peel the cooked potatoes, and reserve enough to equal about half the weight of the cooked salt cod

Sliver the garlic cloves and gently heat in the oil. Gently heat the cream.

Mash or purée the salt cod with the oil, cream, and pepper to achieve a texture that suits you.

A smooth purée is preferred by many and is perhaps the easiest. If in doubt, try this method first. Put the cooked salt cod, garlic, and cream (but not the potatoes) in a food processor and purée to a thick, smooth paste. Then add the cooked potatoes and pulse a few times to blend it in.

To make a *brandade* with more texture, reserve about half the cooked salt cod and chop coarsely by hand. Then puree the other half of the cooked salt cod with the other ingredients in a food processor as above. Finally, mix in the reserved, chopped salt cod.

*Salt Cod Brandade
with Melba Toast*

If you fancy lots of texture, then don't use a food processor at all, but mash up the cooked salt cod in a stand-mixer using the paddle attachment. Then add the oil, cream, pepper, and finally the potatoes. Some authors claim this method mimics the original way of making *brandade*—pounding by hand—but I find the result too fibrous; it sticks between my teeth.

With any of these methods, add extra oil and/or cream to make the stiffness of paste you like. Always taste for salt—it needs to be pleasantly salty.

As an appetizer, divide the *brandade* between four to six ramekins. Always serve with extra pepper and lemon wedges. Some sort of crisp toast is also good, either homemade (see below) or commercial Melba toast. Or serve as an amuse spread on small toasts and sprinkle with lemon juice and extra pepper before serving.

NOTES

The amounts of garlic, cream, oil, and potato specified in the recipe should be considered minimum amounts as a guideline. I invariably add a couple more tablespoons of both oil and cream to get the texture I want—like a sort of soft mashed potato. I find this is one of those dishes you need to experiment with over several iterations to get it just right for personal taste.

If I am using old, mature garlic, I like to heat it very briefly in the oil just to take off the pungent, raw edge. Conveniently, the slivered garlic can be heated in the oil in a stainless steel measuring cup placed directly on the burner for a minute or two, just until the garlic starts to go transparent and sizzle. But if I have very fresh, mild garlic in the fall, I don't bother cooking it first. The cream is conveniently heated the same way.

The heating is necessary because refrigerator-cold ingredients are difficult to emulsify. If you have cooked your salt cod ahead of time and refrigerated it, warm it up (stand it over hot water) before making the *brandade*.

To serve four as an appetizer, divide the *brandade* between four standard, 150-millilitre ramekins; to stretch it to six portions, divide it between six smaller, 100-millilitre ramekins. Or to serve as an amuse, fill small toast cups or simply put a dab on small disks of toast.

TOAST CUPS, DISKS, or FINGERS

makes 50 to 60 cups or disks, or 40 to 45 toast fingers

1 white loaf, very fresh, commercial, pre-sliced
vegetable oil for brushing

Preheat the oven to 350°F. Cut the crusts off each slice of bread. For cups or disks, flatten the slices as thinly as possible with a rolling pin (or bottle).

For toast cups
Cut out disks from the flattened slices to match your mini-muffin pans. Brush each disk lightly with oil on both sides, press into the cups of the mini-muffin pans, bake about 20 to 25 minutes or until medium brown, then remove and reserve. Because they will brown at different rates, you will have to remove them sequentially, a few at a time. Leave to cool, and, if necessary, store in an airtight container to keep them crisp.

For toast disks
Cut out your preferred size or shape of disk, brush with oil on both sides, lay on a baking sheet and bake about 15 to 20 minutes or until medium brown. As previously, they will brown at different rates, so you will have to remove them sequentially. Leave to cool, and, if necessary, store in an airtight container to keep crisp.

For toast fingers
Remove the crusts but do not flatten the slices of bread. Cut each slice into 3 fingers, about 2.5 by 7.5 centimetres. Bake about 18 to 20 minutes or until medium brown. As previously, they will brown at different rates, so you will have to remove them sequentially. Leave to cool, and, if necessary, store in an airtight container to keep them crisp.

NOTES

This is the only time I ever buy commercial, sliced, fluffy, white bread for my kitchen. Buy a loaf as fresh as possible: fresh slices flatten more easily than older and drier slices. The yield will vary from loaf to loaf. Typically there are about 14 usable slices—discard the end slices that are all or partly crust—and typically you can cut four disks from each slice, or three unflattened fingers from each slice.

Mini-muffin pans are widely available, typically with 12 or 24 small receptacles.

Cut the disks as desired or according to the size of your mini-muffin pan. I use a 45-millimetre-diameter cutter for my 45-millimetre mini-muffin pan receptacles.

For flat disks, choose a size suited to the purpose. I find 40 to 45 millimetres a useful general-purpose size.

Use a pastry brush to oil each disk or finger. Any lightly flavoured, neutral vegetable oil can be used, such as a light olive oil, avocado oil, or sunflower oil.

It's a rare oven that will cook a tray of disks or fingers all at the same rate (your best chance is a fan-assisted oven), so check them just before the minimum time and remove any that are done. Then put the rest back in the oven and check them frequently thereafter, removing a few each time, until all are done.

I often buy salt cod just to make *brandade*, but frequently have a little surplus cooked salt cod from some other dish. So I often make a small batch of *brandade*—not only is it delicious in its own right, but it lends itself to other dishes like the following two.

Eggs Benedict is a familiar brunch dish: poached eggs on slices of ham on a toasted English muffin with hollandaise sauce. But this is frequently confused with the similar dish Eggs Benedictine, where the poached eggs sit on a layer of *brandade*. The latter, to my mind, is the better dish.

The names, although almost homonyms, are from completely different sources. Eggs Benedict is a thoroughly American invention, named after a Mr. and/or Mrs. Benedict—there are at least three claimants for this honour. Benedictine on the other hand, is completely French, named after St. Benedict or the Benedictine monks. All French dishes which are *à la Benedictine* have salt cod or *brandade* as a component, in reference to the monks' strict observance of Lent by eating salt cod rather than meat.

This dish depends on careful timing of the components. I strongly recommend you practice by first making this for only two people, halving all the ingredients.

EGGS BENEDICTINE

serves 4 as a brunch main course

4 English muffins
8 eggs
1 batch hollandaise sauce (recipe below)
1 batch brandade
milk or cream to thin the brandade

Split the muffins in half horizontally. Bring a wide saucepan full of water to a boil and add salt. Heat the *brandade* with a little milk or cream. Make the hollandaise sauce. Warm four plates.

Toast the muffin halves, put two halves on each plate, and spread each half with a portion of warm *brandade*, leaving a slight depression in the top to hold the egg that is coming.

Poach the eggs in the salted water, put a poached egg on each *brandade*-covered muffin half, and drape hollandaise sauce over the top of each. Serve immediately.

NOTES

In an ideal world, I would make my own English muffins, but I usually use store-bought; and it's much easier if the *brandade* is made ahead of time and reheated for this dish.

The eggs will take 3 or 4 minutes to poach, so try to get the muffins toasted just before the eggs are ready, to give you a brief window to put *brandade* on each half. To do this, you need to be familiar with how long your toaster takes to brown a muffin—if necessary, sacrifice one ahead of time to find out.

Brandade—particularly if it has been refrigerated—will thicken up as it stands, so adding a little milk or cream as it is reheated brings it back to the right consistency.

Poach the eggs your favourite way, or follow my method. Bring about 3 litres of water to a boil in a shallow, wide saucepan (I use a 30-centimetre pan), add salt (about 1 teaspoon per litre of water), then turn down to a very low simmer with the lid off. Break your eggs into individual little bowls or cups before the water boils, then gently slide each egg into the simmering water, starting at 12 o'clock and sliding in the rest in clockwise order.

After about 2 minutes, start nudging the edge of the saucepan occasionally, looking in particular at the first egg you put in, for that moment when the white has coagulated but still trembles. Usually it's necessary to detach each egg from the bottom of the pan by sliding a very thin, flexible metal spatula under it. Remove the eggs individually with a slotted spoon in the order they went in. Blot the water off each egg by pressing the spoon onto a kitchen towel, then gently slide an egg onto each *brandade*-covered muffin-half.

The fundamental trick to poaching eggs is to have really fresh eggs, so the whites don't flow sideways all around the pan, but stay in a supporting mass around the yolk. If your widest saucepan will not hold eight eggs, use two smaller pans.

ollandaise sauce should be in every cook's repertoire—it's not diffi-cult, it just demands that you pay attention. There are many different ways of making it; here is mine.

BASIC HOLLANDAISE SAUCE

makes about 250 ml

1½ tbsp white wine vinegar
1½ tbsp white wine
3 egg yolks
150 g butter
salt and pepper to taste

Cut the butter into about 12 little slabs.

In a small saucepan, simmer the vinegar and wine on a low heat until reduced to a thick syrup, but be careful not to dry it out and burn it. Take the pan off the heat and whisk in the egg yolks.

Put the saucepan back on a very low heat, and whisk in the slabs of butter, adding each as the last one melts and incorporates itself.

When all the butter has been added and incorporated, continue heating very gently until the sauce has thickened to the desired consistency. Taste and adjust the season-ing. Ideally, serve at once, but if it must be kept waiting for other components, stand the saucepan in lukewarm (not hot) water.

A nd another way of using *brandade* is to make fish cakes.

BRANDADE FISH CAKES

serves 4 as a main course

500 g brandade
250 g onion
2 tsp oil
150 g fresh bread crumbs

½ tsp salt, or to taste
½ tsp pepper, or to taste
70 g dry bread crumbs
2 tbsp ghee, plus extra as needed
  (recipe below)

Cut the onion into small dice. Spread the dry bread crumbs in a shallow tray or on a work surface.

Fry the onions in the oil on low heat until soft, translucent, and lightly browned. Mix the *brandade* with the cooked onions and fresh bread crumbs. Add salt and pepper to taste. Refrigerate the mixture before handling it further.

Divide into eight portions, shape each into a thick disk, press both sides of each into the dry crumbs.

Heat a frying pan on medium heat, add the ghee, then according to the size of your frying pan, fry two to four of the fish cakes for 3 or 4 minutes per side or until richly golden brown. Keep these warm while you fry the remaining fish cakes.

NOTES

Note that both fresh bread crumbs (*in* the fish cakes) and dry bread crumbs (to *coat* the fish cakes) are used in this recipe; the two types have different characteristics, so do not substitute one for the other.

The amounts of fresh bread crumbs and onion are strictly suggestions. The onion is there to add flavour, and the fresh bread crumbs are simply to stiffen the *brandade* to make it possible to handle—add crumbs until the mixture feels right, and bear in mind that chilling the mixture will firm it up considerably.

It is essential to taste the mixture and add salt and pepper, because you will have added salt-free ingredients.

I use a 30-centimetre-diameter cast-iron frying pan, which holds four of these fish cakes comfortably.

Because all the components are already cooked, the final frying is just to brown the outside and warm the fish cakes through.

Both here and elsewhere I strongly recommend ghee for frying any kind of fish or fish cake because it has the desirable flavour of butter without the tendency to burn. Because it keeps indefinitely in the fridge, I always have it on hand.

GHEE

makes about 350 g

500 g butter

Melt the butter in a medium saucepan, and bring to a low boil. Simmer on the lowest heat for up to about 50 minutes. When you become accustomed to the procedure, it can be speeded up or slowed down by adjusting the heat during the process.

If you are in a rush, some or all of the fat can be decanted as soon as it has separated from the watery portion at the bottom, but it won't have the nutty taste of ghee.

Finally, carefully pour off the fat, let cool, and then refrigerate.

NOTES

The principle is that the water in the butter is driven off by sustained heating, leaving the milk solids that were dissolved in that water to brown by further heating, giving the fat fraction a hint of a nutty flavour.

At first, as the watery fraction of the butter sizzles at the bottom of the pan, a white scum gathers on top, which can be skimmed off now, or left to be caught in the final straining. At this stage, it is important to keep the heat *very* low, because the watery part in the bottom of the saucepan will violently erupt occasionally and splatter you if you're not careful.

After about 20 to 30 minutes, the solids at the bottom of the pan will start to colour—pull the surface scum to one side to give you a view through the liquid butter, and tip the pan to see the solids crusting at the bottom.

After about 40 to 50 minutes, the solids in the bottom of the pan will be chocolate brown, and the whole pan will smell nuttily fragrant.

The final separation of the fat from the residual brown debris can be done two ways. Either very carefully decant the liquid fat through a very fine-mesh sieve into a storage jar. Or, pour the fat and any loose browned bits into a paper coffee filter set over a jar and let it trickle through until the filter is cool enough to gently squeeze with your fingers to drive the last drop of fat through the filter. Discard the paper filter and any debris in it.

The solid, chilled, fat fraction is very stable and can be stored in the refrigerator for months, or frozen for long-term keeping.

Most of the salt cod-eating nations have some version of a dish involving onions and potato in a white (béchamel) sauce, like the Portuguese *bacalhau com natas*.

SALT COD in BÉCHAMEL SAUCE

serves 4 as a main course

250 g salt cod, cooked, trimmed weight
250 g onion, trimmed weight
2 garlic cloves
350 g potatoes, trimmed weight
2 tbsp oil

For the béchamel
50 g butter
3 tbsp flour
500 ml milk
1 tbsp Dijon mustard
½ tsp nutmeg
¼ tsp pepper
¼ tsp salt

For the topping
25 g dry bread crumbs
1 tsp oil or melted butter
25 g old, white cheddar
15 g parmesan

Soak, poach, and trim the salt cod as per the Introductory Notes. Slice the onion into one-quarter circles. Chop the garlic finely. Cut the potatoes into about 1.5-centimetre cubes. Grate both cheeses finely. Gently fry the dry bread crumbs on a low-medium heat with the teaspoon of oil or butter, turning them around frequently, until they are lightly browned. Preheat the oven to 350°F.

Make a béchamel sauce from the butter, flour, and milk. Add the mustard, nutmeg, pepper, and salt.

Fry the sliced onion in 1 tablespoon of the oil on a medium heat until soft and lightly browned. Add the chopped garlic for the last minute. Reserve.

Poach the potato cubes in salted water until barely cooked—about 6 to 7 minutes—then drain. Fry the cooked cubes in the other tablespoon of the oil on a medium heat for about 8 to 10 minutes, turning frequently, until all cubes are lightly browned on a couple of sides.

Chop the cooked salt cod coarsely, and mix with the onions, potatoes, and béchamel. Spread this evenly in a baking dish.

Mix the fried bread crumbs with the grated cheeses and sprinkle evenly over the top.

Bake about 45 minutes or until lightly browned on top.

NOTES

For notes on making béchamel sauce, see Cod Hot Pot. To make a richer sauce, substitute cream for all or part of the milk.

Salted water is about 1 teaspoon of salt in 1 litre of water.

A useful size of baking dish is 20 by 20 centimetres, or equivalent.

Frying the bread crumbs before putting on top of the dish helps the topping brown attractively. If the topping does not brown, turn on the broiler for the last few minutes of baking.

The Italian word *frittata* has become thoroughly assimilated into the English-speaking culinary vocabulary, basically meaning a type of open-faced omelette including any of a variety of additional ingredients. This is one of my favourite frittatas.

SALT COD FRITTATA

serves 4 as a lunch main course

250 g salt cod, cooked, trimmed weight
300 g onion, trimmed weight
1 tbsp olive oil
200 g potato, trimmed weight
2 garlic cloves
8 eggs
½ tsp salt
**2 tsp ghee (or butter) to grease
   the frying pan**

Soak, poach, and trim the salt cod as per the Introductory Notes. Slice the onion into thick one-quarter-circles. Chop the garlic finely. Cut the trimmed potatoes into 1-centimetre cubes. Chop the cooked salt cod coarsely. Beat the eggs with the salt. Preheat the oven to 400°F.

Fry the onions on high heat until browned, adding the garlic for the last minute. Poach the potato cubes in salted water until just soft (about 6 to 7 minutes), then drain.

When ready for final preparation, mix together the cooked onions-garlic, the cooked potato cubes, and the chopped salt cod. Stir this gently into the beaten eggs.

Heat an ovenproof frying pan on a medium-high heat, then grease it generously with ghee (or butter). Pour in the egg mixture and immediately start pulling the cooked bits away from the edges with a fork, to let uncooked egg mixture flow into the space. Also stick the fork into the middle of the pan and push the mixture to one side, allowing uncooked egg to flow onto the bottom of the pan. After about 2 minutes of this, put the whole pan into the oven for about 7 to 10 minutes, or until the surface of the mixture is *almost* set with no free liquid egg sloshing about. Don't wait for it to set completely—it will be overcooked.

To serve, either slice the frittata directly in the frying pan, or (better) turn it out on a board and cut into wedges.

NOTES

Here, a thick slice of onion is about 5 millimetres. Fry them as per the method outlined in Salt Cod, Potato, and Onion Casserole.

Salted water for poaching potatoes is about 1 teaspoon salt in 1 litre of water. The best potatoes for this dish are waxy and lower starch, such as the yellow-fleshed variety, but any potato can be used. If you are uncertain of your potatoes, poach an excess weight of them—300 grams whole weight for example—in their skins, peel them when cool enough to handle, then cut into the required 200 grams of 1-centimetre cubes.

I use a well-seasoned, 24-centimetre, cast-iron frying pan for this, and never have trouble turning out the frittata. For notes on ghee, see Salt Cod *Brandade* Fish Cakes.

SALT COD and CHICKPEA SALAD

serves 4 as a lunch main course

300 g salt cod, cooked, trim weight
600 g chickpeas, cooked, drained weight
4 garlic cloves
½ tsp salt
1 tsp pepper
4 tbsp olive oil
2 tbsp lemon juice

Garnish
2 green onions
lettuce leaves (optional)

For comments on soaking, poaching, and trimming salt cod see the Introductory Notes. Ideally the chickpeas and salt cod should be still warm. If they have been refrigerated, warm them slightly. Coarsely flake the salt cod. Slice the green onions thinly on the diagonal.

Mix the warm chickpeas with the warm salt cod.

Mash the garlic with the salt, pepper, and 1 tablespoon of the oil. When well pulverized, add the rest of the oil and the lemon juice. Toss this with the chickpea-salt cod mixture. If it stands before using, toss again just before dividing into portions.

Scatter sliced green onion over each serving.

NOTES

A convenient way to warm cold chickpeas is in a microwave, but chilled salt cod is better heated in a bowl set in a puddle of hot water; stir frequently.

To mash the garlic, either use a garlic press, or sliver the cloves thinly and mash in small bowl or mortar.

I always soak and boil dry chickpeas for this and other recipes. To end up with about 600 grams of cooked, drained-weight chickpeas, start with around 250 grams of dry. If you use canned chickpeas, a regular 540-millilitre can contains about 375 grams drained-weight chickpeas.

The terminology of long-necked, green-topped, small salad onions with narrow bulbs is confusing. Here I call them green onions, but other people call them spring onions, scallions, or even shallots.

Salt Cod and Potato Salad

For me, salt cod is unappetizing when cold straight from the refrigerator, but is delicious in room-temperature salads like the three below.

SALT COD and POTATO SALAD

serves 4 to 6 as a lunch main course

500 g salt cod, cooked, trimmed weight
1 kg baby yellow-fleshed potatoes,
  whole, untrimmed weight
150 g carrot, trimmed weight
50 g red onion, trimmed weight
4 to 6 eggs
4 tbsp mustard vinaigrette,
  plus more to taste (recipe page 66)
salt to taste
pepper to taste

Garnish
chopped parsley, optional

Boil the whole baby potatoes in salted water until tender. Drain, then peel and remove any eyes when cool enough to handle. Cut the trimmed potatoes in half (or quarters if large) to make bite-sized pieces. Gently turn these over, while still warm, in about 2 tablespoons of vinaigrette.

Shred the trimmed carrot using a mandoline (with 2 by 2-millimetre cutter), knife, or coarse grater. Poach these about 30 seconds in boiling salted water, drain, refresh with cold water, drain again, blot dry, and mix with the dressed potato.

Hard boil the eggs, peel, and cut each into four or six wedges.

Taste a small piece of the cooked salt cod to check the saltiness. Toss with a little salt and pepper to taste. Put about 125 grams (for a larger portion) or 85 grams (smaller portion) of cooked, seasoned salt cod in the centre of a soup plate, drizzle or brush with a little vinaigrette.

Pile the potato and carrot around the salt cod on each plate. Arrange wedges of hard-boiled egg around the plate.

Slice the red onion thinly and sprinkle over the potato and carrot on the plate.

Drizzle a little extra vinaigrette over the egg wedges, potato, or fish as liked.

NOTES

As usual, the salted water to boil the potatoes and poach the carrots is about 1 teaspoon of salt per litre of water. If you cannot find baby potatoes, use regular-sized ones and cut them into bite-size pieces after boiling them, either peeled or in their skins.

If you cannot find red onion, use very thinly sliced raw shallot, or a mild onion such as a Vidalia.

For comments on hard boiling eggs, see Salt Cod, Potato, and Onion Casserole.

SALT COD and AVOCADO SALAD

serves 4 as a lunch main course

350 g salt cod, cooked, trimmed weight
4 small avocados, each about 100 g
  whole weight (or 2 larger avocados)
8 to 12 tbsp basic or rouille mayonnaise,
  to taste (recipe page 67)
salt to taste
pepper to taste

Soak, poach, and trim the salt cod as per the Introductory Notes. If the cooked salt cod was refrigerated, warm it, then flake into fork-size pieces.

Trim the avocado, cut into 1-centimetre cubes.

Fold the avocado cubes with about 2 tablespoons of mayonnaise, then mix with the salt cod. Add more mayonnaise to taste. Taste the mixture, and add salt and pepper if desired.

NOTES

For comments on warming chilled salt cod, see the previous recipe.

VINAIGRETTE
general purpose

makes about 9 tablespoons

6 tbsp olive oil
2 tbsp vinegar
1 tbsp Dijon mustard
¼ tsp salt
¼ tsp pepper

Put all the ingredients in a jar (500 millilitres is a useful size) with a tight-fitting lid and shake vigorously until the mixture has emulsified and does not separate when left to stand.

NOTES

The mixture will be difficult to emulsify if the ingredients are cold, so if they have been kept in the refrigerator, bring them to room temperature before making the vinaigrette.

The oil and vinegar are in the standard vinaigrette proportion of 3 to 1. Any vegetable oil can be used, but I like the slightly fruity-peppery taste of a high-quality olive oil—it's worth buying small quantities of top-of-the-line olive oil just for salad dressings.

I particularly like cider vinegar in a general-purpose vinaigrette, but any vinegar can be used, or even lemon or lime juice (but note that balsamic vinegar is sometimes not acidic enough). This basic vinaigrette can be varied ad infinitum to suit different purposes and tastes by slightly altering the proportions and qualities of the oil, vinegar, and mustard, and by adding various combinations of chopped herbs to complement whatever it is going to dress.

BASIC MAYONNAISE

makes approximately 300 ml

1 egg yolk
1 tbsp Dijon mustard
½ tsp salt
¹⁄₁₆ tsp cayenne

250 ml vegetable oil (olive, sunflower,
or avocado oil; or mixed oils)
2 tsp vinegar (white wine or cider)

HORSERADISH MAYONNAISE

makes about 180 ml

½ batch basic mayonnaise
½ tbsp Dijon mustard

2½ tbsp prepared horseradish

ROUILLE MAYONNAISE

makes approximately 300 ml

1 batch basic mayonnaise
4 cloves garlic
¼ tsp cayenne
½ tsp paprika

First make the basic mayonnaise. Whisk together the egg yolk, mustard, salt, and cayenne. Make sure they are warm. Add the oil drop by drop at first, whisking continuously. Then after you estimate you have added about 2 tablespoons by this method, increase the flow of oil to a very thin, intermittent trickle, again whisking continuously. After you have added about half the oil, the mixture will get quite stiff and gelatinous, at which point whisk in the vinegar to thin it. Whisk in the rest of the oil in an intermittent trickle.

If making horseradish mayonnaise, simply mix the ingredients together very well.

If making rouille mayonnaise, sliver the garlic thinly and mash with a pestle in a mortar, or squeeze through a garlic press; mix well with the other ingredients.

Then in all cases, scrape out into a container and refrigerate until needed.

NOTES

There are two keys to making mayonnaise successfully. Ignore them at your peril, because you risk having your mixture curdle or break, two terms for when the mixture fails to emulsify and separates into oil flecked with egg yolk particles.

First, the ingredients must be warm, ideally slightly higher than room temperature. If they are cold, stand your bottle of oil and the mixing bowl containing the egg yolk-mustard mixture in warm (not hot) water. Second, the oil must be added very slowly at first—literally only 2 or 3 drops at a time—until an emulsion has clearly formed in the mixing bowl.

To see if your mixture has failed to form an emulsion, stop whisking for a minute. If the mixture looks particulate, it has failed. But you can salvage your mistake. Gently warm the failed mixture over warm water. Take a fresh egg yolk, warm it, and whisk it in a clean bowl. Then add the failed mixture drop by drop while whisking continuously, then trickle in any remaining oil from your first attempt.

Mayonnaise and its variants should be in every cook's repertoire. Rouille—so called because of its rusty colour—is particularly complementary to a variety of fish dishes.

Chapter Three

HALIBUT

Hippoglossus hippoglossus

HALIBUT

Simply Baked Halibut

Halibut Escabeche

Blackened Halibut

Halibut Thermidor

Halibut in Spicy Coconut Sauce

Potato-Crusted Halibut

The Atlantic Halibut, to use its full name, is the biggest flatfish in the world when full grown, reaching well over 3 metres in length and weighing in excess of 250 kilograms, but such huge specimens are rare these days. It is a creature of the northern, cold North Atlantic and is prized as a food—supporting my general thesis that the colder the water, the tastier the fish.

INTRODUCTORY NOTES ON HALIBUT

Should you be lucky enough to acquire a whole, fresh halibut, it's easy to fillet. But more likely, you will have a choice: halibut steak on the bone, or ready-filleted, skin-on halibut. Choose the latter. Inspect your halibut portion(s) for any remaining bones and remove as necessary. Slide a long, thin knife between the skin and flesh at the narrowest end of the piece, pin down the edge of the skin with one hand, and slide the knife between skin and flesh. Discard the skin (or freeze it to make fish stock later), then remove the pink-grey fatty tissue. This is now fully trimmed.

Many cooks are nervous about cooking fish in general for fear of under- or over-cooking it, and halibut in particular is less forgiving of being over-cooked. The first recipe below is a good one on which to hone your timing skills. Obviously, the cooking time will depend on the thickness of your piece of fish, so take careful note of that. Try sticking a small skewer (I use one about 10 centimetres long, sold for trussing turkeys) through the un-cooked fish to get a sense of what raw feels like. Then stick the skewer in after 10 minutes cooking, and every 5 minutes thereafter, and build up an understanding of what fish undercooked and cooked just right feels like.

Rather than reaching for the frying pan when presented with some very fresh fish of any species, try this simple bake—it works well for any fish.

SIMPLY BAKED HALIBUT

serves 4 as a main course

600 to 700 g halibut, trimmed weight
50 g butter
1 tsp pepper
½ tsp salt
1 tsp paprika, mild or smoked (optional)

To serve
vegetables of your choice

Trim the halibut as per the instructions in the Introductory Notes and cut into 4 equal portions. Preheat the oven to 350°F. Melt the butter and mix in the salt, pepper, and paprika.

Brush a little of the butter mixture on a baking sheet, lay the halibut portions on top, then brush the rest of the butter mixture over the tops and sides of the fish.

Bake about 15 to 20 minutes, or until cooked.

Serve with vegetable accompaniments of your choice. I like a red pepper-onion mixture, with boiled baby potatoes with chives.

NOTES

Including a little paprika imparts an attractive colour, but leave it out if you prefer, and simply use butter, salt, and pepper. And by all means use smoked paprika if you like a slightly smoky edge.

See the Introductory Notes about using a small skewer to test when done.

Escabeche is often confused with ceviche (both words have the same Spanish origin), but the practical distinction in the kitchen is clear: the former is food that is fried then marinated, and comes from the Old World, while the latter is raw food which is pickled or cooked by the action of cold citrus juice, and comes out of South America.

This is one of the best room-temperature fish appetizers. A slightly larger portion also makes a splendid lunch main course.

HALIBUT ESCABECHE

makes 6 appetizers or 4 lunch main courses

350 g halibut, trimmed weight
olive oil for frying fish

For the marinade
35 g carrot, trimmed weight
70 g onion, trimmed weight
1 large garlic clove
3 tbsp olive oil
⅓ tsp salt
⅓ tsp pepper
¼ tsp dry thyme
¹⁄₁₆ tsp cayenne
2 tbsp sherry (or wine) vinegar
1 tbsp white wine
3 small bay leaves

To serve
salad of your choice

Trim the halibut as per the instructions in the Introductory Notes, and cut it into same-size cubes, about 20 to 25 grams each. Coarsely grate the carrot. Coarsely chop the onion. Finely mince the garlic. Mix the vinegar and white wine.

Sweat the carrot, onion, and garlic in 3 table-spoons of olive oil until soft; do not brown. Take off the heat and mix in the salt, pepper, thyme, and cayenne.

Fry the cubes of halibut on medium heat in a little olive oil, turning once, until lightly browned on two sides. Put the cooked fish in a wide, shallow storage container with a tightly fitting lid. Cover the cooked fish cubes with the vegetable and seasoning mixture. Tuck the bay leaves among the fish.

Sprinkle the vinegar-wine mixture over the fish and vegetables. Cover tightly and refrigerate for at least 24 hours, but ideally 5 or 6 days. Gently turn the mixture over every day, being careful not to break up the fish—or invert the tub briefly if you are confident the lid is leak-proof.

To serve, assemble salad of your choice on four or six plates, and divide the cubes of fish between them. Spoon a little of the onion-carrot mixture with some vinegary juices over the top.

Serve with crusty French bread.

NOTES

A non-stick frying pan is useful for the initial frying of the fish. There is no need to brown all sides of each chunk of fish—just get at least two sides lightly coloured. Alternatively, brush the fish with olive oil and bake in a single layer in a 350°F oven about 15 minutes or until just cooked through (see Introductory Notes for testing doneness).

I find sherry vinegar particularly successful in this recipe, but white wine vinegar is fine. Neither balsamic nor rice vinegar are as good. If you prefer this dish a little sharper, use a full 3 tablespoons of vinegar and omit the white wine.

The ideal shape of container for the mixture holds the fish in one layer.

Paul Prudhomme, an exponent of Creole and Cajun cooking, popular-ized blackened fish in the 1980s. He originally used redfish, but the technique has been adapted for use with many different species. The idea rapidly became a restaurant and domestic favourite, and although there are now zillions of recipes for this, the spice mixture doesn't vary much: all seem to include both powdered garlic and powdered onion—two in-gredients I almost never use except for this recipe.

BLACKENED HALIBUT

serves 4 as a main course

600 to 700 g halibut, trimmed weight
50 g ghee (or butter)

Spice mixture
3 tsp paprika
3 tsp onion powder
1½ tsp garlic powder
1½ tsp pepper
1½ tsp dry thyme
1½ tsp dry savoury (or oregano)
¾ tsp cayenne
⅜ tsp salt

To serve
rice and vegetables of your choice

Mix all the spice mixture ingredients and spread out on a baking sheet. Trim the halibut as per the instructions in the In-troductory Notes. Cut the halibut into four equal portions, blot dry with paper towel, and firmly press both sides of each portion into the spice mixture. Reserve the spiced fish on a separate baking sheet. Preheat the oven to 350°F.

Heat a cast-iron frying pan on medium-high heat for about 5 minutes. Put the ghee in the hot pan and push it around with a spat-ula as it rapidly melts. Lay two spiced hali-but portions in the pan and cook about 30 seconds, turn over and cook about another 30 seconds, or until both sides are black-ened but not burnt. Reserve on a baking sheet. Blacken the other portions similarly. Reserve on the same sheet.

Put all the blackened portions in the oven for 5 to 10 minutes, or until just cooked.

Serve with, for example, savoury saffron rice, cauliflower puree, or asparagus spears.

NOTES

The spice mixture is enough for at least six portions of halibut, so the recipe can easily be expanded to that number.

Many recipes dip or brush the fish in melted butter before pressing on the spice mixture. I find this doesn't work because the cold fish congeals the butter into a hard, brittle crust, which easily cracks off and takes the spices with it.

It's possible to get around this by holding the fish at warm room temperature before dipping in butter, but I get very nervous leaving fish lying around in the warmth, and much prefer to press the spices directly on the cold fish, and put the ghee or butter in the hot pan.

Getting the pan just hot enough to properly blacken the fish without excessive burning is a matter of experience. If you find you have produced a thin layer of charcoal on the fish, the pan is too hot. On the other hand, if the fish has only lightly seared after about 30 seconds cooking, the pan was not hot enough. The first indication of the proper pan temperature is the vigorous smoking of the ghee or butter as it melts almost instantaneously in the pan. But if the pan is too hot the fat will vaporize as it melts—and those fat vapours can easily catch fire, so be very careful.

Usually when frying on a hot pan, butter should be avoided because it burns so easily. But here, since everything is going to blacken anyway, it can be used with impunity. But I still prefer to use ghee. Ghee generates fewer fumes than butter, although both will smoke extravagantly on the very hot pan. So never attempt this without an efficient extractor fan—or, even better, do it outdoors, particularly on your first attempts when there may be a risk of a conflagration. For notes about making ghee, see Salt Cod *Brandade* Fish Cakes.

I keep an old cast-iron frying pan just for this purpose. If you think you are going to cook blackened fish regularly, I recommend you do the same; they can often be picked up very cheaply at garage sales.

See the Introductory Notes about using a skewer to test when fish is cooked.

This next recipe is a derived from Lobster Thermidor, a name that stems from the French Revolutionary calendar, which started the year at the fall equinox. This meant that the 11th month was more or less high summer—roughly our July 20 to August 19—and was named Thermidor (from the classical Greek) for the heat of the season.

But exactly where and when the name Thermidor was applied to food is not certain. Some food historians ascribe it very specifically to Maire's, a former restaurant in Paris, where it was invented on the evening of the premiere in 1894 of a play called Thermidor by Victorien Sardou. But others say it was invented in the Café de Paris by chef Léopold Mourier, and there is also an opinion that it was simply applied to dishes when referencing the heat of the mustard they contained.

Whatever the origin, such dishes seem to have fallen out of favour these days, I suspect because too many cooks used too much cheap mustard which pushed dishes over the thin line between pleasantly piquant and aggressively hot.

But I very much like the flavour of mustard, provided of course the cook uses a quality mustard and adds it judiciously. Monkfish is also good prepared this way—simply substitute monkfish for halibut in this recipe.

HALIBUT THERMIDOR

serves 4 as a main course

600 to 700 g halibut, trimmed weight

For the sauce base
100 g shallot, trimmed weight
100 g leek, trimmed weight
100 g celery, trimmed weight
100 g carrot, trimmed weight
50 g butter
160 ml dry white wine
160 ml fish (or chicken) stock

To finish the sauce
milk as needed
75 g butter
4 tbsp flour
2 tsp tarragon
2 tbsp fresh parsley
3 tbsp Dijon mustard
½ tsp salt
½ tsp pepper
2 tsp dry vermouth

For the topping
40 g Gruyère
20 g dry bread crumbs

Trim the halibut as per the instructions in the Introductory Notes, and cut into same-sized chunks, about 20 to 25 grams each. Coarsely chop the shallot, leek, carrot, and celery. Finely grate the Gruyère, and mix with the dry bread crumbs, breaking up any clumps of cheese. Preheat the oven to 350°F.

Sweat the chopped vegetables in the 50 grams of butter on low heat until soft. Add the wine and stock, bring to a boil, and simmer on very low heat for about 30 minutes. Strain this, pressing down hard on the solids in the sieve. Reserve the fluid, and discard the solids.

Melt the 75 grams of butter in a medium saucepan. Whisk in the flour and cook on low heat for 5 minutes. Make up the reserved fluid to 500 millilitres with milk. Whisk this into the flour and butter, raise the heat, and whisk until thickened. Whisk in the tarragon, parsley, mustard, salt, pepper, and vermouth. Then simmer on very low heat for 10 minutes.

Mix the chunks of fish with the sauce, and transfer to a 20 by 20-centimetre baking dish. Smooth the top and sprinkle the cheese-bread crumb mixture evenly over the top.

Put the dish in the oven for about 20 to 25 minutes. Turn on the broiler for the last few minutes to brown the topping.

Serve at once.

NOTES

Both here and elsewhere, note that when cutting up the fish, it's more important to get similar-sized pieces, rather than any particular size, so they all cook in the same time.

White pepper rather than black is often recommended because the latter leaves the sauce with black speckles. I think white pepper has a different taste, so I always stick with the black—and the speckles get lost among the flecks of tarragon and parsley.

The time spent under the broiler will depend on how hot your broiler is. Alternatively (or in addition) it's a good idea to toast the bread crumbs before mixing with the cheese; see the notes under Cod au Gratin.

Halibut in Spicy Coconut Sauce

Perhaps surprisingly for such a delicate fish, I find that halibut lends itself particularly well to spicy flavours. Here is one of my favourites.

HALIBUT in
SPICY COCONUT SAUCE

serves 4 as a main course

600 to 700 g halibut, trimmed weight

Spicy coconut sauce
300 g onion, trimmed weight
4 garlic cloves
40 g fresh ginger, trimmed weight
4 tbsp oil
4 green serrano peppers
1 tsp turmeric
350 g coconut milk
**350 g tomatoes, fresh or canned,
    trimmed weight if fresh**
1½ tsp salt

Coarsely chop the onion. Finely chop the ginger and garlic. Slice the whole hot peppers as thinly as possible crossways, discarding the stalk. If using fresh tomatoes, remove the skins. Chop either fresh or canned tomatoes coarsely. Trim the halibut as per the instructions in the Introductory Notes and cut into same-size chunks.

Fry the chopped onion, ginger, and garlic in the oil on low-medium heat until soft but not browned. Add the sliced hot peppers and turmeric and fry gently for another 5 minutes.

Add the chopped tomatoes, coconut milk, and salt to the onion-hot pepper mixture. Bring to a boil and simmer on low heat about 20 minutes to meld the flavours. Use immediately or refrigerate if keeping overnight.

Choose a wide, shallow saucepan that can hold the halibut cubes in one layer. Reheat the sauce in that saucepan, spread out the cubes of fish in the sauce, and gently bring the sauce to a low simmer. Cover the pan and gently simmer about 5 minutes, then turn the cubes over and cook for another 2 to 4 minutes or until the fish is just cooked through.

Serve at once with rice, accompanied by western-style vegetables or Indian accompaniments such as dal, raita, and chutneys.

NOTES

While I like the flavour that fresh hot peppers provide, I am not fond of intensely hot peppers. It's really a matter of balancing flavour and heat, hence my preference for a variety from the middle of the hotness spectrum: green serranos in this case. According to your own preferences, use one to four or more serranoes, or a hotter pepper such as habanero.

But whichever hot pepper you choose, be very careful when cutting them. Rather than chopping them, I simply slice whole peppers very thinly while holding them down by the stalk end. After handling them, be very careful not to touch some delicate body membrane—do not rub your eyes, for example—until you have thoroughly scrubbed your hands, and even then some very hot peppers will linger on your fingers long enough to provide a painful surprise. Which is why some people wear disposable vinyl gloves when handling hot peppers.

Purists may prefer to make their own coconut milk, but I find a quality canned coconut milk is better than I can make myself, given the vagaries of locally available coconuts. In particular I find the small 160-millilitre cans particularly useful: two such cans are close enough for this recipe.

If you can find good, well-flavoured, fresh tomatoes, then use them. But peel them, because the skins can be intrusive. To peel tomatoes, drop them into rapidly boiling water, leave for 15 to 20 seconds, then immediately plunge them into cold water. Then strip off the skins. Also remove the cores if the tomatoes are large, but for this recipe don't bother deseeding them. Often the best option is a quality brand of canned, peeled tomatoes; a 400-millilitre can will give you the right amount for this recipe. Whichever you use, chop them coarsely before adding.

This dish is all the better for having the spices mellow and meld overnight. Ideally, make the sauce the day before and cook the fish in it the next day.

POTATO-CRUSTED HALIBUT

serves 4 as a main course

600 to 700 g halibut, trimmed weight
400 g potatoes, trimmed weight
2 eggs
2 pinches salt
150 g flour
½ tsp salt
½ tsp pepper
4 tbsp ghee (or oil) to fry, plus more
  as needed

Suggested accompaniments
parsnip puree
snap peas

Trim the halibut as per the instructions in the Introductory Notes, and cut into 4 equal portions. Julienne the trimmed potatoes on a mandoline into 2 by 2-millimetre shreds. Dump the shreds into a bowl of cold water. Mix the flour with the ½ teaspoons of salt and pepper (this mixture is seasoned flour) and spread on a plate. Beat the eggs with pinches of salt and pour onto a plate. Lay a piece of waxed paper (or parchment) on your work surface. Preheat the oven to 350°F.

Drain the potato shreds in a sieve, roll in a kitchen towel and squeeze as dry as possible. If the towel gets soaking wet, repeat with a second, dry towel.

Pat the halibut portions dry with paper towel. Dredge them in the seasoned flour, shake off the surplus, then dredge in the beaten egg and lay on the waxed paper. Press dry potato shreds onto each side of each portion of fish, pressing the potato firmly against the fish.

Heat a frying pan on medium-high heat and add 2 tablespoons of ghee (or oil). Lay one of the potato-crusted portions of fish in the hot frying pan and fry for a total of about 3 to 4 minutes, carefully turning it over at half-time. The potato on each side should be well browned, but unless the fish is very thin, it will not be fully cooked at this stage. Reserve on a baking sheet.

Remove any burnt bits of potato that have fallen off the fish into the pan, add a little more of the ghee, and fry the other portions of potato-crusted fish in similar fashion.

Put the baking sheet with the potato-crusted fish in the oven for about 5 to 10 minutes or until just cooked through.

Serve immediately with the suggested accompaniments or whatever you fancy.

NOTES

Any potato can be used, but I find russets ideal for this recipe. About 700 grams whole weight will yield about 400 grams of blotted-dry shreds.

If you have no mandoline to shred the potatoes, grate them on the coarse side of a box-grater. It's important to get grater-cut potato shreds into cold water as soon as possible because they will turn black quickly—the grater bruises them as it cuts, which leads to premature blackening.

This can be cooked without the egg wash, but the potato layer tends to detach from the fish. But a little potato will fall off anyway, both in the preparation and in the frying pan.

The cooking time of the fish will vary according to thickness. Test with a small skewer as per the Introductory Notes. For notes on ghee, see Salt Cod *Brandade* Fish Cakes.

Chapter Four

HERRING, SALT and SMOKED

Clupea harengus

SALT HERRING

Pickled Herring

Soused Herring with Potato Salad

SMOKED HERRING (KIPPERS)

Poached Kippers au Naturel

Kippers and Coddled Eggs

Kippers, Avocado, Lentil, and Beet Salad

SALT HERRING

Salt herring were once an important component of the Newfoundland economy but are now much diminished as a commercial product and have largely fallen out of favour domestically.

Salt herring can still be found at some retail outlets, and the quality is usually good, but don't buy them if the fish has rust-coloured stains, or if they smell in the slightest of rancid oil, or if they look old, dry, and tired. Search for the largest you can find, preferably at least 200 grams each (salted weight). Very often you will have to make do with smaller ones, but in general don't bother with salt herring that are less than 100 grams each. In the ideal world, you will salt your own herring, choosing the freshest, largest, and fattest fish.

At the most basic level, salt herring can be simply soaked, simmered, and put on a plate. All very well, but there are more interesting things to do with them, which fall into two broad categories, both of which start with soaking and filleting. In the first category these prepared fillets are cold-soaked in vinegar; in the second they are simmered in vinegar. Unfortunately, there is much confusion in the terminology attached to these two categories. The terms pickled or soused seem to be applied indiscriminately to both—and also to similar treatments of fresh herring. Here, I use the term pickled to mean soaked, salt herring immersed in a cold vinegar mixture for days, and soused for soaked, salt herring briefly cooked in a vinegar mixture.

PICKLED HERRING

makes 12 fillets of pickled herring

6 salt herring, whole, large if possible
250 g onion, trimmed weight
175 g carrot, trimmed weight
2 tbsp black peppercorns, whole
2 tbsp allspice berries, whole
8 bay leaves
600 ml vinegar
150 ml water
125 g sugar

To serve
thinly sliced rye, multi-grain,
   or whole-wheat soda bread
sour cream
thinly sliced red onion
garnishes as desired,
   such as alfalfa sprouts

Soak the salt herring about 24 hours in fresh water, changing the water three or four times. Then fillet the herring and remove all the large bones but leave the smallest. Rip off the skin and tidy up the fillets. Thinly slice the carrot and onion. Dissolve the sugar in the vinegar and water—stir until the sugar is completely dissolved.

In a non-reactive container, spread a thin layer of the sliced vegetables, then layer the trimmed fillets with the rest of the sliced vegetables and spices. Cover with the vinegar-sugar solution and leave to soak in the refrigerator for at least 2 days, preferably more.

To serve, spread sour cream on a piece of bread, lay some thin slices of red onion on top, and then a fillet of pickled herring—either whole or cut into four or five pieces—with other garnishes as liked.

NOTES

The fillets can be eaten after only 2 or 3 days of pickling time, but are best left at least 7 days, and will be at their optimum after about 10 days.

I particularly like cider vinegar or sherry vinegar in this recipe. Most vinegars can be used, but I avoid both balsamic vinegar (not acidic enough) and industrial white vinegar (too aggressively acidic).

My preferred bread for this is a dense, dark, thinly pre-sliced, rye bread, but a thin slice of whole-wheat soda bread is also excellent. The sour cream and red onion are essential, unless you dislike raw onion, but all other garnishes are to taste.

Served with salad, this makes a nice lunch dish—serve two fillets for larger appetites—or an appetizer before a lighter main course at dinner.

SOUSED HERRING with POTATO SALAD

makes 12 herring rolls

6 salt herring, whole, large if possible
250 ml cider vinegar
250 ml dry white wine
65 g sugar
2 tsp coriander seeds, whole
2 cloves, whole
1 cinnamon stick, about 7 cm
2 red chilis, dried, whole
1 bay leaf
2 tsp black peppercorns, whole

To serve
potato salad made with vinaigrette
  or mayonnaise
garnishes to taste

Soak the salt herring in water for about 24 hours, changing the water three or four times. Fillet, debone, and trim, but leave the skin on.

Roll up each fillet, starting at the thick end with the skin outside, and secure with a small non-reactive skewer.

Bring the vinegar, wine, and all spices just to a boil in a non-reactive saucepan, drop in the rolled herring fillets, put on the lid, turn off the heat, and let stand until it has cooled to room temperature. Then remove the rolls and refrigerate.

To serve, let the refrigerated rolls come back to room temperature, remove the skewers, and place two or three in the middle of a dish. Surround them with potato salad and garnish to taste.

NOTES

A non-reactive saucepan invariably means stainless steel these days, but make sure your stainless pan doesn't have aluminum rivets fixing the handles to the saucepan and its lid—the aluminum will corrode in the acidic vapours of the hot vinegar.

The skewers here must be able to withstand cooking in vinegar. I like small (10-centimetre) stainless steel ones, usually sold for trussing turkeys. Lacking those, use bamboo toothpicks, sharp and tough enough to withstand being pushed through the tough skin of the fish—but don't leave your hand on the other side or you will skewer that as well.

Which potato salad to use is a personal choice; for me this dish suits the mayonnaise style. For notes on mayonnaise see Salt Cod and Avocado Salad. If you prefer a vinaigrette dressing, see the notes under Salt Cod and Potato Salad.

For garnish I favour slivered green onions, chopped red onion, and cherry tomato halves.

SMOKED HERRING
(KIPPERS)

Kippered herrings—kippers for short—seem like an ancient food, something that began way back in human history and evolved slowly over the centuries. Not so; they were invented in the 1840s, when enterprising manufacturers on the coast of Northumberland (England) decided to adapt a salmon-smoking technique called "kippering" for herring.

From a very early age I have loved kippers. So when I arrived in this land of fish I assumed that here they would be both good and plentiful. I was cruelly disappointed. Almost all the commercial kippers here were (and are) very poor examples.

The problems were legion: too small, too salty, too dry, too smoked, too tough, or all of the above. But things are improving, because excellent kippers are to be had here these days if you can buy them from a small artisanal smoker or know an experienced amateur smoker who will give you a few.

But whatever the source, look for larger kippers, preferably 250 grams (split, smoked, head-off weight) and 200 grams at a minimum. Don't bother with smaller specimens; they will usually be too dried out.

Most kipper recipes start with cooking them and taking the meat off the bones, so the following recipe for Kippers *au Naturel* is in fact the start of many other recipes. If you are eating them in this style in company, you will probably want to use a knife and fork, but if the kippers are being prepared in the kitchen for a subsequent dish, use your fingers as the primary implement.

If you are *sure* your kippers are lightly salted and delicately smoked—that is, made by an individual or small firm that cares—then by all means grill them or roast them on the barbecue. But the best general-purpose way to cook kippers from any source is to poach them.

POACHED KIPPERS AU NATUREL

serves 2 to 4 at breakfast, lunch, or dinner

4 kippers, at least 250 g each, head-off, whole weight
4 l water

To serve
whole-wheat bread, whole-wheat soda bread, or whole-wheat sourdough bread, and butter

Bring the water to a full rolling boil in a saucepan wider than the kippers are long, with a lid.

Slide no more than two kippers into the boiling water, put the lid on the saucepan, turn off the heat and leave for 5 minutes (or 6 if they are big kippers—300 grams plus). Remove them from the pan immediately.

Do not cook for very much longer than these recommended times because secondary bones will start to detach from the backbone and be more difficult to remove. Drain the kippers briefly and keep warm while the other two are being cooked. Serve on warm plates with artisanal whole-wheat bread of some sort, and butter.

NOTES

If the kippers are just slightly too long for your widest saucepan, don't be afraid to cut off the tails to make them fit: this will not affect the following procedure.

Taking apart kippers needs practice, even more than most procedures in the kitchen. As I have said, the first step to success is not overcooking them, so that major rib bones stay attached to the backbone and are discarded with it.

If you are going to eat the kipper right away, lay it on a warmed plate. If the kipper meat is to be reserved for another use, lay it on a small plastic cutting board—the smell of kipper juice can offensively permeate a wooden board. A cold kipper is much more difficult to dismember than a warm one, so don't be tempted to refrigerate it before taking it apart.

Lay the kipper skin-side up in front of you: head-end to your left, tail-end to your right—or vice versa. Carefully separate the edge of skin nearest you from the underlying meat. Remember that kippers are split along the back, so you will have the bases of the dorsal fins on one (or both) long edges; detach any rows of fin bones you encounter.

As you lift the edge of the skin, gently push the fillet of meat down and away from the skin until you see the line of grey-brown fatty tissue. Then either detach this fatty tissue from the flesh, or leave it attached if, like me, you like to eat it. Gently lift the fillet of meat off the underlying bones in one or more pieces. Push and lift the skin to reveal the next fillet, then lift this off the underlying bones in a similar fashion.

Then turn the kipper around so the other edge of skin is toward you, and repeat the process.

Some people prefer to tackle the kipper skin-side down, following a similar procedure, but if you are inexperienced, try skin-side up first. Either way, try to catch all the larger bones at this stage. There will always be little hair-like bones you miss, but they don't matter; part of the reason to eat substantial whole-wheat bread with kippers is to mask such finer bones.

If the meat is to be reserved for later use, cover and refrigerate it. A typical 250-gram whole kipper will yield about 100 grams of kipper meat.

Eggs are natural partners to fish in general, and smoked fish in particular, as illustrated by this recipe. Unusually, I can remember where I got this idea: from an erstwhile colleague, Ian Ball, who called it Coldstream Eggs, and claimed that the Coldstream Guards (a British army regiment— one of the few that wear bearskin hats) liked them after a chilly night of sentry duty.

I strongly suspect this is yet another food-history myth, and Ian is now dead, so I cannot question him further. I have seen Coldstream Eggs associated with food in Cornwall, but that's as far as I've gotten with the provenance of this recipe.

But no matter, the concept is excellent, and I like it very much, although I have tweaked Ian's original recipe.

KIPPERS and CODDLED EGGS

serves 4 at breakfast or lunch, or as an appetizer at dinner

**100 g kipper meat, cooked,
 trimmed weight**
½ tsp Worcestershire sauce
½ tsp pepper
3 tbsp cream, plus more if needed
4 eggs
4 pinches salt
butter to grease ramekins

To serve
bread, or toast fingers

Cook a kipper and reserve the meat. Preheat the oven to 350°F. Have a kettle of boiling water on standby. Generously grease 4 ramekins.

Coarsely chop the kipper meat and mix with the Worcestershire sauce and pepper, then mix in enough of the cream to make a stiff paste. Divide this between the greased ramekins, pressing the mixture down into each, and leaving a shallow depression in the mixture with the back of a teaspoon.

Carefully break an egg into each depression in the kipper mixture in each ramekin, being careful not to break the yolk. Put a pinch of salt on top of each egg. Cook in a *bain-marie* in the oven for about 20 minutes.

Serve as a breakfast dish, light lunch with a salad, or an appetizer at dinner, with bread or toast of your choice.

NOTES

To get the required 100 grams of trimmed-weight kipper meat, start with about a 250-gram kipper, whole weight. For notes on cooking and dissecting a kipper, see Kippers *au Naturel*.

A useful size of ramekin for this recipe is around 150 millilitres, about 7.5 by 3.5 centimetres, diameter by depth.

When chopping the kipper meat, watch for any large bones you may have missed. It's a good idea to use a kitchen tweezers to pick them out. But ignore the very fine, hair-like bones.

If you do break the yolk when adding the egg to a ramekin, carefully tip out all the egg, leaving the kipper mixture in the ramekin, and try again with another egg.

If you are unfamiliar with baking things in a *bain-marie*, see the notes under Smoked Cod Custards.

Bake until the egg is done to your liking. The timing is critical if you want a runny yolk and just-set white. The top of the egg should be opaque and should gently wobble when you reach into the oven and nudge the water bath. But there are many variables at play here: the exact temperature of your oven; the initial temperature of the egg, and the temperature of the kipper mixture, all of which affect the cooking time. Therefore, I urge you to make an experimental batch and cook them one at a time, to get the hang of what your preferred state of doneness looks like, before launching a full batch on your public.

KIPPERS, AVOCADO, LENTIL, and BEET SALAD

serves 4 as a lunch main course

100 g kipper meat, cooked,
  trimmed weight
2 avocados, ripe
200 g beetroot, cooked, trimmed weight
150 g lentils, preferably French,
  cooked weight
vinaigrette to taste
salt to taste
pepper to taste

Garnish
parsley, or other garnishes to taste
  (optional)

Cut the avocados in half lengthways, remove the pits, and peel off the skins. Brush with a little of the vinaigrette to prevent discolouration if they are not going to be used immediately.

Chop the cooked beetroot into 1-centimetre cubes. Mix with the cooked lentils. Add 3 or 4 tablespoons of vinaigrette, or to taste. Season with salt and pepper to taste. Divide this between four small bowls, creating a small depression with the back of a spoon in the top of each pile to receive an avocado half. Press an avocado half into each.

Break up the kipper meat with your fingers or chop coarsely. Divide this between the four avocado halves, piling it carefully in and over the pit cavity. Dribble about ½ teaspoon of vinaigrette on each pile of kipper meat. Sprinkle with chopped parsley, or garnish of your choice (optional).

NOTES

To get the required 100 grams of cooked kipper meat, start with a 250-gram whole kipper. For notes on cooking and dissecting a kipper, see Kippers *au Naturel*.

When breaking up the kipper meat, watch for and remove any larger bones you may have missed in the initial trimming.

This makes four portions, but with another avocado it can be stretched to six slightly smaller servings.

The best lentils for this dish are the mottled green French (Puy) lentils. Green or brown lentils can be used if you are *very* careful not to overcook them, which makes them mushy, but do not use red lentils—they will fall apart.

To get about 150 grams cooked-weight French lentils, start with about 75 grams dry weight. To get about 200 grams cooked weight beetroot, start with about 350 grams whole beetroot.

For notes on making vinaigrette, see Salt Cod and Potato Salad.

Kippers, Avocado, Lentil, and Beet Salad

Chapter Five

MACKEREL

Scomber scombrus

MACKEREL

Smoked Mackerel Soufflé

Smoked Mackerel Spread

Smoked Mackerel
and Leek Quiche

The mackerel is a beautiful and elegant fish. Because of Newfoundland and Labrador's cold ocean and bountiful supplies, mackerel (like herring) should be the best in the world here, and easily available. And they are, if you catch them yourself, or have an angling friend willing to give you some.

The problem is that mackerel deteriorate very rapidly once out of water. This has long been recognized, and is why they could be sold on the Sabbath in the streets of 18th-century London (England) despite the general ban on Sunday trading.

So if you try to buy fresh mackerel from the supermarket, be extremely cautious. Despite the protestations from behind the counter—"Oh yes, really fresh, absolutely fresh, came in just this morning!"—you are unlikely to find them fresh enough in a commercial retail outlet. Therefore, because most people most of the time will have no access to truly fresh mackerel, I do not consider them here. Just in passing I will say that one of the best ways to eat them is filleted, grilled hot and fast on a barbecue, and served with a sharp sauce: rhubarb, partridgeberry, or the traditional gooseberry (interestingly, the French call gooseberries *groseille à maquereau*—mackerel berries).

But smoked mackerel is a different matter. Mackerel stand up to the abuses wreaked on them by commercial smokers better that herring do, making it worth your while to try any you come across. Fortunately, we now have artisanal producers in the province making some of the best smoked mackerel I have encountered anywhere.

INTRODUCTORY NOTES ON SMOKED MACKEREL

Smokers of mackerel make either a hot- or cold-smoked product, or something somewhere on the spectrum between the two, between fully cooked and raw that is. Once you are familiar with them, they are easily distinguished by eye; if in doubt, poke a fillet with a fork: the hot-smoked mackerel flakes apart easily.

The recipes I give here all start with cooked, smoked mackerel. If that's what you have, simply trim the fillets: remove skin, fins, and bones, and pick off the bulk of the grey-brown fatty tissue which lies along the outside of each skinned fillet.

But if you have cold-smoked, uncooked fillets, slide them into 4 litres of boiling water, turn off the heat, and let sit in the pan, covered, for 15 minutes. Then take them out, and when cool enough to handle, trim them similarly.

A large, 12-gram untrimmed fillet of smoked mackerel will yield approximately 75 grams of trimmed-weight meat.

SMOKED MACKEREL SOUFFLÉ

serves 4 to 6 for lunch, or 6 to 8 as an appetizer at dinner

75 g smoked mackerel, cooked, trimmed weight
50 g butter, plus extra for greasing the dish
4 tbsp flour
250 ml milk
1 tbsp Dijon mustard
½ tsp Worcestershire sauce
¼ tsp salt
¼ tsp pepper
4 egg yolks
6 egg whites
Pinch cream of tartar

Preheat the oven to 400°F. Generously butter a soufflé dish. Coarsely chop the trimmed mackerel.

Make a thick béchamel sauce with the butter, flour, and milk. Whisk in the mustard, salt, pepper, and Worcestershire sauce. Reserve off the heat.

Stir the chopped mackerel into the béchamel, then stir in the yolks.

Whip the whites with the cream of tartar to soft peaks. Stir a big dollop (about 125 millilitres) of this into the béchamel mixture, then fold in the remainder of the whipped whites.

Pour and scrape this into the buttered dish, smooth the top, and score a circle in it.

Put the filled dish in the oven, on a baking sheet in case it overflows, and immediately turn down the heat to 375°F. Bake about 45 minutes, or until well risen and golden brown.

Serve immediately.

NOTES

For advice on cooking, trimming, and calculating the yield of smoked mackerel, see the Introductory Notes. For notes on making béchamel sauce, see Cod Hot Pot.

The initial dollop of whipped egg white should be stirred into the béchamel quite vigorously—the purpose is simply to thin the sauce slightly to make the subsequent folding easier. The rest of the whipped egg white should be folded in, not stirred.

Folding is an essential kitchen technique: push a flexible, silicone (or rubber) spatula flat-side down under the mixture, lift it up, and put what you have lifted on top of the rest of the mixture. Repeat until the mixture looks fairly homogeneous.

It's important to butter the inside of the soufflé dish generously, both to help the rising mixture slide up the sides of the dish, and to create an appetizing brown crust on the sides of the soufflé.

A soufflé will rise in virtually any shape of dish, but ideally use one designed for the purpose. Such dishes are typically about three times wider (diameter across the top) than deep. The one I use regularly is 20 centimetres diameter, 7 centimetres deep.

After roughly smoothing the top of the mixture in the dish, score a line by running your spatula around the mixture 3 to 4 centimetres in from the rim; this helps the rising soufflé to break along that line and make an attractive crown when baked.

SMOKED MACKEREL SPREAD

makes 50+ amuse portions, or serves 6 as an appetizer

250 g smoked mackerel, cooked, trimmed weight
75 g butter
25 g red onion
25 g celery
25 g sour gherkins
¼ tsp pepper, plus extra to taste
1/16 tsp cayenne
salt to taste
oil to grease ramekins

Appetizer accompaniment
avocado-grapefruit salad (see below) or a salad of your choice

Make sure the butter is room temperature soft. Finely chop the onion, celery, and gherkins. Coarsely chop the smoked mackerel.

Mix the chopped mackerel with the butter, chopped onion, celery, gherkins, pepper, and cayenne. Taste, and add salt and pepper as needed.

Oil six small ramekins, including the top rim, and line each one with plastic film. Divide the mixture between the lined ramekins, squashing the mixture down so that the plastic is pressed firmly against the ramekin. Fold the surplus plastic over the top of the mixture, and refrigerate.

To serve as an appetizer, bring the ramekins to room temperature, lift up the folded-over flaps of plastic, lift out each portion in its cradle of plastic film, and invert onto the centre of a plate. Garnish the plate with salad.

To serve as an amuse, spread a small portion of the mackerel mixture on toast cups or disks.

NOTES

For advice on cooking, trimming, and calculating the yield of smoked mackerel, see the Introductory Notes. It's usually necessary to chop rather than simply mash the mackerel because the smoking process leaves a thin, tough layer on the outside of the flesh. And the chopping gives you another chance to remove any residual bones.

Salt may or may not be needed, depending on the saltiness of the mackerel; taste the finished mixture.

For notes on vinaigrette, see Salt Cod and Potato Salad.

A small ramekin is about 100-millilitre capacity (about 6 by 3.5 centimetres, diameter by depth).

Oiling the ramekins prevents the plastic film clinging to the ramekin and becoming impossible to slide against the sides.

For notes on making toast cups or disks, see Salt Cod *Brandade*.

AVOCADO-GRAPEFRUIT SALAD

serves 4

2 small red grapefruit
3 small avocados
vinaigrette
parsley to sprinkle

Remove the skin of the grapefruit, including all the white pith. Cut down alongside the membranes separating the segments and remove the segments of flesh. From two small grapefruit you should get around 30 segments. Peel the avocados and slice into at least 30 thin wedges (i.e., 10 or 12 per avocado). Chop the parsley. Arrange five wedges of avocado around each little drum of mackerel spread, put grapefruit wedges between them, sprinkle with vinaigrette and then with chopped parsley.

Both eggs and leeks are natural complements to fish in general, and smoked fish in particular.

SMOKED MACKEREL and LEEK QUICHE

makes one 23-centimetre quiche

one 23 cm precooked savoury-pastry
   tart shell, waterproofed (recipe below)
100 g smoked mackerel, trimmed weight
150 g leeks, trimmed weight
15 g butter
2 eggs

170 ml cream
2 tsp Dijon mustard
¼ tsp salt
¼ tsp pepper
⅛ tsp nutmeg

Preheat the oven to 350°F. Coarsely chop the trimmed mackerel. Slice the trimmed leeks into 1-centimetre logs.

Sweat the chopped leek in the butter until completely soft and limp; reserve.

Beat the eggs with the cream, mustard, salt, pepper, and nutmeg. Stir in the cooked leeks, breaking up any clumps. Stir in the chopped mackerel meat. Carefully scrape this mixture into the precooked pastry shell.

Bake about 40 minutes, turning the tart around at half-time, or until well browned on top.

Eat hot, warm, or at room temperature.

NOTES

For advice on cooking, trimming, and calculating the yield of smoked mackerel, see the Introductory Notes.

If your smoked mackerel is particularly salty, use only ⅛ teaspoon salt.

When trimming the leeks, discard the dark green parts, keeping only the pale green and white bits.

SAVOURY PASTRY
general purpose

makes two 23-centimetre tart shells or equivalent

300 g flour, plus more to dust
¾ tsp salt
150 g cold butter
50 g cold lard, or vegetable shortening
6 to 7 tbsp cold water

Egg wash to waterproof the shells if
needed; enough for two 23-centimetre
shells
1 whole egg
1 pinch salt

Mix the salt with the flour. Cut the butter and lard into 1-centimetre cubes and place on top of the flour mixture. Chill for at least an hour. Then transfer it to the bowl of a food processor and pulse the mixture until the fats are all reduced to small pieces no bigger than a split pea (or cut them into the same size with a hand-held pastry cutter).

Turn out the processed mixture into a large bowl. While swirling the mixture with a large fork in one hand, sprinkle the water over the mixture with the other, 1 tablespoon at a time. Only use the last tablespoon of water if the mixture doesn't start to hold together.

Turn out onto the work surface, gather the mixture together, and gently press it into a block. Cut in half and press one half down on top of the other. Repeat this manoeuvre two or three times until it is holding together (but at this point will still be a little crumbly). Divide into two equal portions, squashing each portion into a round, flattened disk, pressing together any crumbly bits as you do so. Wrap in plastic film, and use the wrapping process to push the dough together. Refrigerate at least 3 hours, preferably overnight. One (or both) portions can now be frozen for future use.

Remove one portion of dough from the refrigerator and leave at room temperature about 45 to 60 minutes before attempting to roll it. Then unwrap the dough and lay it on a lightly floured work surface. Dust your hands and the rolling pin with flour, and start rolling from the centre of the disk of dough to the edge, rotating the dough about 45 degrees between strokes of the rolling pin.

As you start the rolling process, pinch together the dough as it forms little cracks around the perimeter. Keep the dough an even thickness as you roll it. Keep the work surface and rolling pin well floured to prevent it sticking. If it does stick slightly, slide a long, narrow spatula between the pastry and the work surface to release it.

Roll the dough according to its intended use. For a 23-centimetre tart shell, roll out the dough until a 30-centimetre circle will fit inside the ragged edges of the disk. Gently lift up one edge, drape it over your rolling pin, then rotate the pin to wind the pastry onto it. Position the dough over your tart mould or plate, so that when you un-wind the pastry it is centred on the mould or plate.

Gently push (rather than press) the pastry from the sides to persuade it down into the mould or plate, making sure it's tucked right into the corner. Run a small knife along the rim of the mould or plate to slice off the overhanging pastry. If that disturbs the pastry, gently push it back against the mould or plate. Prick the bottom of the raw pastry all over with a fork. Refrigerate for at least an hour.

Preheat the oven to 375°F. Bake the pastry shell a total of about 40 to 45 minutes, un-til golden brown; bake the first 25 minutes blind.

If the cooked shell is going to be re-cooked with a fluid filling, whisk together the egg and salt to make an egg wash, brush this generously over the base of the cooked shell, and put back in the oven for 2 min-utes.

NOTES

When baking blind, pastry is baked for about the first half of its total cooking time with a piece of foil on the pastry holding about 300 grams of beans or other weights. This is removed for the second half of the baking time.

The final brush with egg wash more or less waterproofs the pastry.

Chapter Six

MONKFISH

MONKFISH

Monkfish à l'Americaine

Monkfish in Fermented
Black-Bean Sauce

Monkfish in Mild Curry Sauce

Monkfish with Madeira Sauce

Monkfish on the Barbecue

Monkfish is unmistakable: from above, you see primarily a big, circular head, with a broad, toothy mouth and a pair of fins and a tail stuck on as an afterthought. The species occurs along the eastern seaboard of North America, where it has never been appreciated as much as the nearly identical species found along the eastern Atlantic coasts is appreciated by Europeans.

It's a sit-and-wait predator, embedding itself in the seabed, where its colouration affords excellent camouflage while it waits for prey. The most anterior of the spines on its head is waved around in front of its mouth. Unwary, small fish attracted by this "bait" are engulfed by the fish's huge mouth—hence one of its alternative names: angler fish. But despite its unprepossessing appearance, the meat from the tail is excellent.

INTRODUCTORY NOTES ON MONKFISH

Usually what you see for sale is the tail, either in one piece with the central backbone, or two fillets. Either way, the outer skin is usually removed, but the membranes between skin and flesh left in place: they are labour intensive to remove, so commercially are usually left in place for the customer to struggle with.

Occasionally, the whole fish is offered for sale, at a greatly reduced price because so much of it is head. It looks daunting, but don't be afraid to buy the whole thing. Ask the fishmonger to cut the tail from the head, use the tail in any of the recipes here, and make a fine fish broth with the chopped-up head.

However you buy monkfish, take care to remove all the slippery membranes and the bulk of the areas of dark-coloured flesh from the surface of the meat. All these are perfectly edible, but will contract during cooking and distort your neat pieces of fish.

Many people have observed that monkfish has the texture of lobster; not surprisingly monkfish takes well to lobster recipes, like the first two below. In addition, note that the recipe for Halibut Thermidor—derived from Lobster Thermidor—works very well with monkfish, as does Halibut in Spicy Coconut Sauce. In both cases, simply substitute monkfish for the halibut in the recipe.

This recipe is adapted from the well-known Lobster *à l'Americaine,* where rich lobster meat is complemented by tomatoes, garlic, olive oil, and cognac.

Food historians, well known for strong opinions based on weak evidence, have fallen out over the origin of this name. But the evidence—unusually—appears clear cut: the authoritative *Larousse Gastronomique* says the name was coined for an impromptu lobster dish prepared around 1860 in Paris by Pierre Fraisse, a French chef who had worked in America, and named his new dish after that country.

MONKFISH à l'AMERICAINE

serves 4 as a main course

600 to 700 g monkfish, trimmed weight
30 g ghee (or butter)
4 tbsp cognac

For the sauce
100 g shallot, trimmed weight
50 g carrot, trimmed weight
2 garlic cloves
3 tbsp olive oil
125 ml white wine
500 g tomatoes, untrimmed,
  whole weight
125 ml fish stock
2 tbsp cognac
4 tsp tarragon
½ tsp salt
¼ tsp pepper
⅛ tsp cayenne

Finely chop the shallot. Finely grate the carrot. Finely mince the garlic. Peel and core the tomatoes, leave the seeds in place, and chop them into 0.5-centimetre dice. Trim the fish as per the Introductory Notes, then cut into same-size pieces, around 20 to 25 grams each. Preheat the oven to 350°F.

Sweat the shallot, carrot, and garlic in the olive oil until soft. Add the white wine and reduce to a glaze. Add the chopped tomatoes, fish stock, the 2 tablespoons of cognac, tarragon, salt, pepper, and cayenne to the saucepan. Simmer until the tomatoes are soft, then take the lid off the saucepan and reduce the sauce until little free liquid is left and the sauce has thickened. Reserve.

Warm the cubed fish in the ghee (or butter) on medium heat. Do not attempt to cook the fish completely at this stage, simply heat it in preparation for the next step. Flame with the 4 tablespoons of cognac. Mix with the thickened sauce and put into a 20 by 20-centimetre baking dish with a cover.

Bake about 30 minutes in a covered pan until just cooked.

NOTES

For this dish, make the effort to find a fresh tomato that tastes of tomato—most don't. I use fresh Campari tomatoes. For notes on peeling tomatoes, see Halibut in Spicy Coconut Curry.

When simmering the sauce to thicken it slightly, either judge by eye—simmer until little free liquid is visible—or weigh it: the thickened sauce will be about 225 grams.

For notes on ghee, see Salt Cod *Brandade* Fish Cakes.

Flaming food (flambéing) with alcohol should be a technique in every cook's repertoire, to flame the Christmas pudding if nothing else. The principle is that warm food vaporizes some spirit which is set alight, and it flavours the food as it burns.

In practice, this means having a box of matches or (better) a propane wand-lighter immediately to hand, as well as a small jug of your chosen spirit—usually cognac (or brandy), whisky, or rum. Pour the spirit directly on the hot food and immediately apply a flame. Do not lean over the food as you do so because the whole thing will go up in a whoosh of flame, which soon dies down as the alcohol burns off.

For notes on testing with a skewer to see if the fish is cooked, see Halibut Introductory Notes.

Here is another recipe borrowed from the lobster-cooking canon.

MONKFISH in FERMENTED BLACK-BEAN SAUCE

serves 4 as a main course

600 to 700 g monkfish, trimmed weight
50 g shallot, trimmed weight
2 tsp fresh ginger, trimmed weight
2 garlic cloves
25 g fermented black beans
3 tbsp ghee or oil, plus extra
  to grease pan
¼ tsp pepper
¼ tsp salt
190 ml fish (or chicken) stock,
  plus extra to thin sauce as needed
2 tsp cornstarch
2 eggs
2 pinches salt

Garnish
3 green onions

Trim the monkfish as per the Introductory Notes, and cut into same-size cubes, about 20 to 25 grams each. Finely chop the shallot. Finely mince the garlic, ginger, and fermented black beans. Whisk the eggs individually with a pinch of salt in two separate, small bowls. Blend the cornstarch with about 65 millilitres of the stock. Trim the green onions then slice on the diagonal.

Lightly grease or oil a crepe pan and put on medium heat until lightly smoking. Add one of the beaten eggs, swirl it around to spread it evenly over the pan, leave on the heat until the egg is completely cooked, then turn out onto a cutting board. Repeat with the other egg. When cool enough to handle, roll up each pancake and slice thinly. Reserve.

Select a wide saucepan that will eventually hold the fish cubes in one layer. Fry the shallots in this in the ghee or oil on low heat for about 2 minutes. Add the garlic, ginger, and black beans, and fry on a low heat for another 2 minutes, just to take the raw edge off them. Add the remaining stock, salt, pepper, and cubed monkfish. Bring to a low boil, cover the saucepan, and simmer about 5 or 6 minutes or until barely cooked. Remove the chunks of fish and reserve in a warmed serving dish.

Stir the cornstarch mixture, then pour into the saucepan and heat gently until the sauce thickens and goes translucent. Thin with a little more stock if liked. Mix in the reserved egg slivers and cook briefly just to reheat.

Pour the sauce over the reserved, cooked fish. Scatter the chopped green onions over the top.

Serve with plain steamed rice, steamed potatoes, or pasta of your choice.

NOTES

Fermented black beans can be found in Asian food stores.

Sauces thickened with cornstarch have a very fine line between lightly, pleasantly thickened and too thick and gluey. Add extra tablespoons of stock to thin the sauce as needed.

Do not be tempted to omit the egg: it mellows the assertive flavour of the sauce and complements the fish. But if the beaten egg is simply stirred into the sauce, as some recipes recommend, there is a risk it will simply thicken the sauce rather than set into shreds of cooked egg. Which is why I pre-cook the egg in a 23-centimetre crepe pan into thin omelettes and then shred those.

For notes on testing with a small skewer for when fish is cooked, see Halibut Introductory Notes.

*Monkfish in Fermented
Black-Bean Sauce*

This mild curry sauce is equally good with other white fish. For example, simply substitute an equal weight of halibut for the monkfish in this recipe.

MONKFISH in MILD CURRY SAUCE

serves 4 as a main course

600 to 700 g monkfish, trimmed weight

Curry sauce
¾ tsp black mustard seeds, whole
2 tbsp oil
175 g onion, trimmed weight
15 g ginger, trimmed weight
2 garlic cloves
¾ tsp coriander
¼ tsp turmeric
¼ tsp cumin
⅛ tsp fenugreek
⅛ tsp cayenne
100 ml tomato sauce
¼ tsp salt
3 tbsp water, plus more if needed

To serve
rice or boiled potatoes
Indian dal or spiced vegetable dish,
  or western-style vegetables

Trim the monkfish as per the Introductory Notes, and cut into same-size chunks, around 20 to 25 grams each. Chop the onion into small dice. Finely mince the ginger and garlic. Preheat the oven to 350°F.

Fry the mustard seeds on medium heat in the oil until they start popping, then add the chopped onions and fry until they are soft but not browned. Add the minced ginger and garlic for about the last 5 minutes.

Add the dry spices (coriander to cayenne) and fry for another 2 minutes. Add the tomato sauce, salt, and water. Bring to a boil and simmer on very low heat about 30 minutes. If the sauce seems too thick, add water. Mix the cubed monkfish with the sauce.

Select a baking dish that will accommodate the fish cubes in a single layer, and which either has a lid or can easily be covered with foil. Level out the sauce-fish mixture in this baking dish, put on the lid (or cover with foil), and bake about 30 minutes or until just cooked.

NOTES

Any tomato sauce can be used. I use either my own homemade, or a quality tinned tomato sauce (but not tomato paste), or some Italian passata

sauce. If you have no pre-made tomato sauce, use fresh tomatoes: peel, deseed, and chop enough finely to make the required volume. For notes on peeling fresh tomatoes, see Halibut in Spicy Coconut Curry Sauce.

To judge the thickness of the sauce, drag a spoon across the bottom of the pan. I like it when the sauce is still thin enough to flow back into the furrow, rather than remaining heaped on each side. Add water or evaporate further to suit your taste.

This dish is improved by letting the spices mellow and meld overnight. If time allows, make the sauce the day before and refrigerate overnight before cooking the fish in it the next day.

For notes on testing for doneness with a small skewer, see Halibut Introductory Notes.

This is a lightly peppery dish that works well with other white fish, particularly halibut—simply substitute halibut for monkfish in this recipe.

MONKFISH with MADEIRA SAUCE

serves 4 as a main course

600 to 700 g monkfish, trimmed weight
1 tbsp pepper
1 tbsp flour

1 tsp salt
50 g ghee (or butter)
2 tbsp cognac or brandy

For the sauce
190 ml chicken (or fish) stock
4 tbsp Madeira (or port),
 plus more as needed
6 tbsp cream, plus more as needed
¼ teaspoon salt, or to taste

Accompaniment suggestions
savoury rice
asparagus, or vegetables of your choice

Trim the monkfish as per the Introductory Notes, and cut into same-size chunks, about 20 to 25 grams each. Mix pepper, flour, and salt together to make a highly seasoned flour.

Dredge the trimmed fish cubes in the highly seasoned flour and shake off all surplus. Fry these in ghee (or butter) on a low-medium heat at a gentle sizzle until just cooked, about 10 minutes, turning the pieces over at half-time. Then flame with the cognac, remove the fish, and keep warm.

Add the stock, Madeira (or port), cream, and salt to the frying pan. Boil vigorously to reduce to a thin sauce. Taste frequently, and add more stock, wine, cream, and salt as needed to achieve a taste and consistency you like.

To serve, lay some asparagus spears on a bed of savoury rice, put chunks of cooked monkfish on top, and top with a portion of the sauce.

NOTES

For notes on flaming food, see Monkfish *à l'Americaine*.

As usual, I prefer ghee over butter for frying the fish. For notes on ghee see Salt Cod *Brandade* Fish Cakes.

For notes on testing for doneness with a small skewer, see Halibut Introductory Notes.

This recipe works well with either drier or sweeter Madeiras, and equally well with port.

The firm texture of monkfish makes it ideal for the barbecue because, unlike cod, it doesn't break when turned. Any flat grilling surface can be used for this recipe.

Do not marinate fish for as long as you would beef or chicken, because fish absorbs flavours more quickly—15 to 30 minutes is enough.

In general, keep marinades for fish simple, and don't let citrus dominate because it will pickle the fish before it gets to the barbecue. Experiment, and find combinations that suit you.

MONKFISH
on the BARBECUE

serves 4 as a main course

600 to 700 g monkfish, trimmed weight
oil to wipe the barbecue grates

Marinade #1
2 tbsp olive oil
1 tbsp lemon juice
1 garlic clove
¼ tsp pepper
⅛ tsp salt

Marinade #2
2 tbsp olive oil
1 tbsp lemon juice
1 garlic clove
¼ tsp pepper
1 tbsp dark soya sauce

Marinade # 3
2 tbsp olive oil

1 tbsp lemon juice
1 garlic clove
⅛ tsp salt
1 tbsp tomato ketchup
1 tsp hot pepper sauce

Trim the monkfish as per the Introductory Notes, and cut into same-size chunks, about 20 to 25 grams each. Preheat a barbecue on maximum.

Mix the ingredients for one or more marinades. If the marinade contains garlic, crush or very finely mince it. Each marinade is enough for the full 700 grams of fish, so if using less fish, or making 2 or more marinades, reduce the ingredients proportionately.

Mix the fish cubes with the marinade(s) and leave at room temperature for 15 to 30 minutes.

When ready to cook the fish, thread the cubes on skewers, no more than about six or seven chunks on each, and grill—lid down—until cooked.

NOTES

The ideal skewers are flat-sided, not round, so when the skewer is turned over, the food turns as well, rather than rotating like a wheel on the skewer. They should also be long enough for the handles to stick out well clear of the hot grills so they can be handled easily. I use 35-centimetre, stainless steel, flat skewers.

If you prefer to use wooden skewers, be sure to soak them for an hour beforehand in hot water to help prevent them burning too much.

If you are unaccustomed to grilling fish on the barbecue, here is what I do. Preheat a perforated metal plate—usually sold for grilling vegetables—placed directly on the grates of the barbecue.

When the marinated fish is on the skewers, wipe the preheated metal plate with a little vegetable oil—on a pad of paper towel held in tongs—and immediately lay the skewers of fish on the plate, leaving the handles sticking out beyond where the lid will come down, and put down the lid of the barbecue.

Cook for a total of 5 or 6 minutes, turning once, slightly longer on the first side than the second (3½ minutes and 2½ minutes for example) or until the fish is cooked through.

For notes on testing for doneness with a small skewer, see Halibut Introductory Notes.

SALMON

SALMON

Cold-Smoked Salmon on Dark Bread

Hot-Smoked Salmon Salad

Hot-Smoked Salmon Pâté

Cured Salmon with Beetroot

One of the best memories of my early days in Newfoundland was the seasonal arrival of fresh, wild Atlantic salmon. And what a treat they were! It seems unbelievable that now there is a whole generation (perhaps two) of Newfoundlanders who have never tasted *real* salmon—real *wild* Atlantic salmon that is. Of all the many abject failures of our political classes, I hold their inability to protect the Atlantic salmon (from both other nations and ourselves) among their worst offences. Their excuses, both federally and provincially, have been lessons in mendacious, self-serving, finger-pointing short-termism. A pox on both their houses.

So most of the time, unless you are a fortunate angler who catches their own, we are stuck with farmed salmon, a miserable second-best. I can almost weep to think that this noble creature has been reduced to the fishy equivalent of industrial chicken, simply a source of cheap protein. Occasionally, almost of necessity, I do eat some, but in general try to avoid it like any other inferior foodstuff. So I give no recipes here for fresh, farmed salmon.

However, even farmed salmon becomes palatable if it is processed before consuming, either by smoking with a preliminary salting, or just curing with salt and (usually) sugar.

The commercially and artisanally smoked salmon we can get in Newfoundland, even though almost always made from farmed fish, is as good as any except the very best from Ireland, Scotland, or Scandinavia. We have both excellent hot- and cold-smoked salmon, two quite different processes and products that need different treatments in the kitchen.

COLD-SMOKED SALMON

Cold-smoked salmon is smoked at low temperatures, not hot enough to cook the fish, so the product is essentially raw, although considered to be partly "cooked" by the curing in salt before being smoked.

To my palate, all dishes that involve heating cold-smoked salmon—putting it on hot pasta for example—are a waste of time because they bring out the worst in smoked salmon, emphasizing its fishy oiliness. In general, I do not recommend *any* dish where cold-smoked salmon gets heated.

Apart from a few very labour-intensive preparations where some savoury filling is elaborately wrapped in slices of cold-smoked salmon, there is really only one way to eat it on a regular basis: straight from the refrigerator, thinly sliced, with a complementary garnish to emphasize its best aspects, as in the following recipe.

COLD-SMOKED SALMON on DARK BREAD

serves 10 to 15 as an amuse, or 6 to 8 as an appetizer

**250 g cold-smoked salmon,
  roughly trimmed weight**
4 or 5 slices dark pumpernickel rye bread
sour cream

Garnish
red onion
**or any other garnish of your choice,
  such as sour gherkins, capers,
  or shallots**

Fully trim the smoked salmon, slice it thinly, and reserve in the refrigerator. Cut the bread into your preferred size of squares or rectangles (or circles). Cut the onion into quarters lengthways and sliver one quarter crossways thinly. Or prepare other garnish of your choice.

Put a blob of sour cream on each portion of bread, lay a sliver of red onion or some garnish of your choice on top of the cream, then roll or fold a slice of smoked salmon and place on top. Or place the salmon directly on the sour cream, then glue the garnish to the top of the salmon with a further, tiny dot of sour cream.

NOTES

Cold-smoked salmon never needs much trimming because the process starts with ready-trimmed fillets, what I call the roughly trimmed weight. But some finishing touches are always required. Slice off the thin, fatty belly flap and the fatty rim from what was the back of the fish, but leave the skin on the fillet. Run a finger along the length of the fillet feeling for the ends of pin bones. Commercial smoked salmon will have these (mostly) removed, but home-smoked salmon may have them all in place. Pull out any you find with a small pair of needle-nosed pliers, and keep the pliers handy because you may encounter some buried pin bones as you slice through the fish.

Estimating how many slices you will get is always tricky: it depends on how much you trim from the original slab, and how thinly you can slice the rest. As a rough guide, I find that a 250-gram roughly trimmed piece

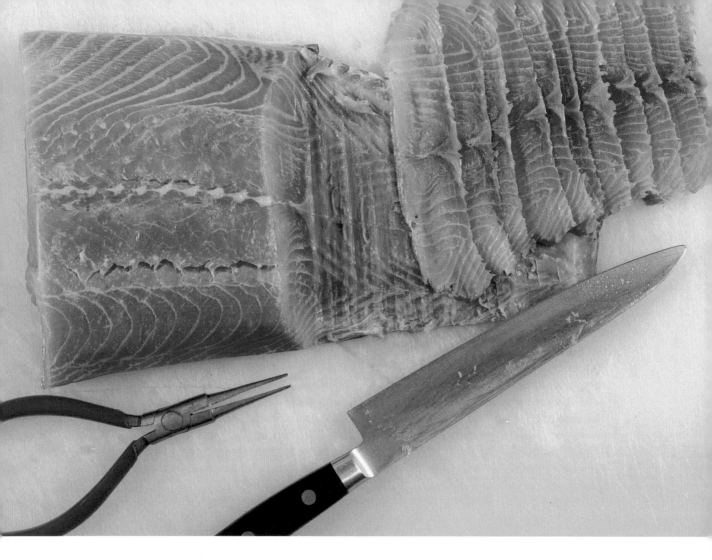

will yield about 215 grams of usable smoked salmon, from which I can usually cut 50+ slices, which will serve 6 to 8 people as an appetizer, or about 10 to 15 people as an amuse.

Cold-smoked salmon is not often sold in pieces as small as 250 grams, so I necessarily buy larger pieces, or a whole side, and cut off enough for immediate needs before freezing the rest. If you have bought a side of smoked salmon already frozen, thaw it slightly to the point where you can just cut it into smaller pieces—but don't thaw it completely—and re-freeze the pieces you haven't used.

Slicing smoked salmon does not require a specialized slicing knife, although if you have one you will no doubt relish using it. Any regular kitchen knife longer than about 15 centimetres will do the job: the only *essential* requirement is that it be as sharp as you can get it. Slice the smoked salmon as thinly as you can with slanting cuts across the fillet. Adjust the angle of the slanting cut to suit the width of slice you want: the closer to vertical you hold the knife, the narrower the slice of salmon.

And contrary to conventional wisdom, it's not necessary to start at the tail end and work your way back to the head end of the fillet. But depending on which end you start, there will usually be a couple of thinner, saltier slices at the tail end, and perhaps a nub left at the head end that is impossible to slice; consider both these cook's perks.

I think the best pumpernickel for this recipe is the almost-black, slightly sticky, dark rye, usually sold pre-sliced; the one I buy has slices about 9.5 by 11.5 centimetres. I cut a slice into 12 small rectangles, about 2.75 by 3 centimetres each—just the right size for eating as one mouthful as an amuse, or for serving six or eight on a plate as an appetizer.

The best sour cream for this recipe is thick, sometimes called "restaurant style." Crème fraiche is a good substitute, as is a thick yogurt, because they have the necessary acidity. Don't substitute stiffly whipped, fresh cream: it's not acidic enough.

According to which garnish you prefer: thinly slice or finely chop red onion (my favourite); thinly slice shallots; drain, rinse and coarsely chop capers; thinly slice sour gherkins, or prepare your preferred garnish in an appropriate fashion.

HOT-SMOKED SALMON

Hot-smoked salmon is processed at a temperature high enough to cook the fish as well as smoke it, which gives it a texture that makes it impossible to slice as one can cold-smoked. But like cold-smoked salmon, it is not improved by including in a hot dish, as is often recommended. The best ways to eat it are as a salad with suitable accompaniments, or mashed into a pâté, as in the recipes below.

INTRODUCTORY NOTE

The hot-smoking process usually leaves the salmon with a thin, dark, tough, outer pellicle. Slice this off and chop it finely, then mix it with the rest of the flesh as per the particular recipe.

HOT-SMOKED SALMON SALAD

serves 4 as a lunch main course

250 g hot-smoked salmon
4 eggs
500 g small potatoes (about 15 to 20)
500 g asparagus
2 avocados
50 g cherry tomatoes (about 6 to 9)
lettuce or cucumber or other greens
  to line a platter (optional)
vinaigrette to taste

Hard boil the eggs. Chop the pellicle of the salmon as per the Introductory Note, and mix with the coarsely flaked flesh. Boil the potatoes (unpeeled) in salted water for about 15 to 20 minutes or until cooked, then drain and reserve until cool enough to handle. Trim the asparagus. Make vinaigrette if you have none on hand. Cut each tomato in half.

Peel the potatoes while still warm, drizzle with a little vinaigrette, and reserve.

Poach the asparagus in salted water until tender, drain, then drizzle with a little vinaigrette and reserve.

Peel the avocados, remove the pits, and slice them lengthways into a total of about 16 strips. Drizzle with a little vinaigrette and reserve.

When cool, cut each boiled egg one into 4 lengthways.

Line a bowl or platter with lettuce leaves, sliced cucumber, sliced zucchini, or whatever you fancy (optional).

Pile the flaked hot-smoked salmon in the centre. Arrange the cooked potatoes around the fish, then arrange the asparagus on top of the potatoes. Put a ring of avocado strips around the perimeter and arrange the egg quarters on or among them. Decorate with tomato halves.

NOTES

For notes on hard-boiled eggs, see Salt Cod, Potato, and Onion Casserole. For notes on making vinaigrette, see Salt Cod and Potato Salad.

As elsewhere, salted water for boiling vegetables (or pasta) is about 1 teaspoon of salt in 1 litre of water.

To trim asparagus, select one of the thicker stalks. Hold it at each end and gently bend it between your hands until the tough, thick end snaps away

Hot-Smoked
Salmon Salad

from the rest. The butt that breaks off will be about one-third of the total length of the stalk. Then line up all the other asparagus stalks and cut off the butts at the same level. Discard these tough, thick butts, or use them to make asparagus soup. Then peel the lower, thicker half of what is left of each stalk; use a vegetable peeler with a serrated blade that will dig into the asparagus skin.

The boiled potatoes are done when a small skewer stuck into the biggest one meets no resistance.

Similarly, poach the asparagus stalks until a small skewer easily penetrates the thick end of a stalk, about 2 to 4 minutes.

The hot-smoking process which makes salmon impossible to slice makes it splendid for mashing, and to my mind this is where hot-smoked salmon really shines.

HOT-SMOKED SALMON PÂTÉ

makes 40+ amuse portions, or serves 4 as an appetizer

**125 g hot smoked salmon,
  trimmed weight**
40 g chèvre
1 tbsp sour cream, plus more if needed
½ tbsp prepared horseradish
salt, to taste
¼ tsp pepper, or to taste
½ tbsp capers, whole
1 tbsp shallot

Salad for appetizer portions
1 red pepper
35 to 40 thin green beans
salt and pepper to taste
vinaigrette to taste
or salad of your choice

Garnish for amuse
any or all of:
slivers of black olive
small rectangles of roasted red pepper
sprigs of parsley
or garnish of your choice

Chop the shallot finely. Rinse, drain, and coarsely chop the capers. Chop the pellicle of the salmon as per the Introductory Note.

Mash the chèvre with enough sour cream to make a malleable paste. Mash in the soft flesh and the chopped pellicle of the smoked salmon, the horseradish, capers, and shallot. Taste and add salt and pepper if needed.

For appetizers, divide the mixture between four small ramekins and press it down firmly, wrap in plastic film, and refrigerate.

To serve as an appetizer, run a small knife between each pâté and its ramekin, carefully lever the contents out onto plates, and serve with a salad.

To serve as an amuse, spoon into toast cups and garnish.

Salad for appetizer portions
Roast the red pepper, then trim and slice into strips the size of the beans. Poach the green beans in salted water until tender, plunge into cold water to stop the cooking, then drain and blot dry with kitchen towel.

Toss the red pepper strips and green beans with vinaigrette, and salt and pepper to taste. Arrange around the portions of salmon pâté on their plates.

NOTES

Do not be tempted to try this with cold-smoked salmon. It doesn't work.

Instead of sour cream, yogurt or fresh cream can be used to make the chèvre malleable.

For different amounts of salmon, use chèvre at one-third the weight of the salmon, and adjust other ingredients in proportion.

Here, a small ramekin is about 75-millilitre capacity, about 6.5-centimetre diameter.

Salted water for poaching vegetables is about 1 teaspoon in 1 litre of water.

By far the best method for roasting peppers is to put them directly in the flame of a gas stove or gas barbecue. As the skin blackens, turn the peppers around to char the entire surface—and really char them, to the point where there are patches of grey ash. When charred all over, drop the peppers in a paper bag, twist the top to close, and leave to steam until cool enough to handle. Then cut out the pepper's stem and core, remove the membranes and seeds from the inside, and scrape off the bulk of the charred skin from the outside. Lacking an open gas flame, peppers can (less successfully) be roasted in a very hot oven.

The salad to accompany the appetizer portions is strictly a recommendation; any of the other salads mentioned in this book can be used.

For notes on making toast cups see Salt Cod *Brandade*. For notes on making vinaigrette, see Salt Cod and Potato Salad.

CURED SALMON
(a.k.a. GRAVLAX)

can exactly pinpoint my first encounter with a cured salmon recipe. It was in that excellent Time-Life Series *Foods of the World*,
which has stood the test of time and, although highly US-cen-
tric, has a wealth of information about other nations. The recipe
in question was for gravlax, that quintessentially Scandinavian
preparation of fresh salmon cured in salt and sugar and flavoured
with dill.

The basic technique is clearly an ancient one, a way of semi-pre-
serving fresh fish, but the idea really only penetrated the interna-
tional cooking scene in the 1960s. Many other countries, France in
particular, enthusiastically adopted the technique, and put their
own twist on it. Most versions of gravlax use a combination of
salt and sugar as the basic cure, but the proportions differ between food cultures: Scandinavians generally prefer more sugar,
while the French tend to let salt dominate.

Dill was the traditional flavouring for gravlax, but the culinary
world has moved on, and all manner of ingredients can now be
found flavouring the salmon. I find that dill, and the traditional
mustard-dill sauce accompaniment, combine to overpower the
taste of the salmon. But many people still think that gravlax auto-
matically means dill, so here I call this dish simply cured salmon.
I think beetroot nicely complements the salmon without overwhelming it.

CURED SALMON with BEETROOT

makes about 100 slices:
serves about 20 to 30 as an amuse, or 12 to 16 as an appetizer

500 g salmon, fully trimmed weight,
** skin on**
50 g coarse pickling salt
50 g sugar
100 g beetroot, raw, trimmed weight
1 tbsp dry vermouth

Garnish
sour cream as needed
100 round, flattened-bread toasts,
** or bread of your choice**

Garnish: raw or vinegared onion
100 g red onion, or as needed
(see recipe page 165)

Buy roughly trimmed, filleted salmon with the skin on. Trim the salmon completely but leave the skin on. Place skin-side down in a baking pan or similar dish that holds it comfortably.

Peel the beetroot and coarsely grate it. Mix the sugar, salt, and grated beetroot. Pat this mixture evenly over the flesh side of the salmon, then drizzle the vermouth over this.

Cover the dish with plastic film and refrigerate. After the first 24 hours, lift the plastic cover occasionally, tilt the pan to swirl the accumulated fluid around, and spoon the accumulated fluids and undissolved sugar and salt over the fillet.

After 72 hours, take the fish out of its marinade, scrape off most of the salt-beetroot mixture, then briefly rinse off any remaining mixture under cold running water. Pat very dry with paper towel, place in a plastic bag, and refrigerate.

To serve, slice the cured salmon, put a dab of sour cream on a round of toast or rectangle of dark bread, put a few strands of either raw or vinegared onion on top, then lay a rolled slice of cured salmon on top of that.

NOTES

For notes on the final trimming of salmon, see Cold-Smoked Salmon. Here, the idea is to end up with a neat, 500-gram, fully trimmed rectangle of raw salmon.

A useful size of dish for this size piece of salmon is an 18 by 28-centimetre glass dish. Many recipes insist on putting weights on the salmon as it cures, but I find this unnecessary.

Ideally refrigerate for at least a day after its curing time before using, but it can be used immediately. It keeps for many days in the refrigerator, so can be made well ahead of time.

For notes on slicing salmon, see Cold-Smoked Salmon.

Rather than dark rye bread (which suits cold-smoked salmon), I think cured salmon is best served on toast disks (see Salt Cod *Brandade*). I find both the sour cream and either type of onion to be essential garnishes, although it does work well without onion.

RAW or VINEGARED ONIONS

100 g red onion
boiling water
1 tbsp brown sugar
¼ tsp salt
65 ml red wine vinegar

For raw red onions, simply sliver the onion thinly.

For vinegared onions, slice the red onion into semi-circles. Cover with an excess of boiling water, stir well, and leave to soak for 5 minutes. Drain well. Immediately mix the sugar, salt, and vinegar with the warm onions, and let stand 10 minutes, turning the mixture over three or four times. Drain and refrigerate until needed.

Chapter Eight

TROUT

Oncorhynchus mykiss,
Salmo trutta, Salvelinus fontinalis, and others

TROUT

Potted Trout

Trout Chowder

Trout with Bacon

Trout Mousse

Trout Mousse Wrapped in Sole

Trout Wrapped in Parchment

For reasons I don't fully understand, farmed trout is less offensive than farmed salmon; they seem to survive the aquaculture process better and end up leaner and less fatty. Try farmed trout in any of these recipes, although wild trout will *always* be better. Any of the local species will work well, and should you be lucky enough to catch and keep—or be given—a wild Atlantic salmon, it can also be used in any of these recipes.

INTRODUCTORY NOTES

When trimming trout, remove all skin, fins, and bones. If using farmed trout in these recipes, it's best to also remove the bulk of the grey-brown fatty tissue from the skin side of each fillet; with wild trout this is not necessary.

Potting fish was originally a method of storing perishable seafood for days or weeks, but these days it's used simply as a way of making a flavourful appetizer out of small amounts of fish or shellfish.

All fish is highly perishable, so do not try to keep any seafood made in the simplified style I describe here for more than a few days, although it's fine to make ahead and keep briefly in the refrigerator.

To keep potted fish for longer periods requires different, more careful techniques. If done properly, this does make something that can be kept for weeks, but do not attempt it without taking expert advice.

This recipe is distinctly better made with wild trout or wild salmon, but worth trying with farmed trout.

POTTED TROUT

makes 75 amuse portions in toast cups, or serves 6 as an appetizer

50 g shallots, trimmed weight
50 g butter, plus extra to grease ramekins
250 g wild trout, raw trimmed weight
  (or use leftover, cooked trout)
1 tbsp white wine
1 tsp dry vermouth
1 tbsp capers
½ tbsp green peppercorns
¼ tsp salt
¼ tsp pepper
⅛ tsp nutmeg

To serve as appetizer portions
6 orange slices to go under each
  trout portion (optional)
toast fingers

horseradish mayonnaise
3 tomatoes to make cups for the
  mayonnaise (optional)

Roasted red pepper salad (optional)
2 red peppers
1 tsp vinaigrette, or dressing
  of your choice
salt and appear to taste

To serve as amuse
toast cups or disks
slivers of black olive, or tomato,
  or garnish of your choice (optional)

Finely chop the shallot. Rinse, drain, and coarsely chop the capers. Rinse and drain the peppercorns, but do not chop. Trim the trout as per the Introductory Notes and cut into same-size chunks. If making a red pepper salad, roast the peppers, chop into 0.5-centimetre dice, dress with a little vinaigrette, and add salt and pepper to taste; reserve.

Grease 6 small ramekins, including the top rims. Cut six 15-centimetre squares of plastic film. If using tomato cups for the mayonnaise with the appetizer, cut the tomatoes in half and scoop out the seeds. Make toast fingers for the appetizers, or toast cups or disks for the amuse.

Sweat the chopped shallot in the butter until soft but not browned. Add the wine and vermouth, and reduce to a glaze. Add the trout, cover the pan, and cook on very low heat until the fish is cooked through (about 5 to 10 minutes according to thickness). If you are using leftover pre-cooked trout from some other dish, omit this step.

When the trout is cooked, chop it up with a wooden spatula right in the saucepan. Do not reduce it to a purée—leave some coarse texture.

Add the chopped capers, whole peppercorns, salt, pepper, and nutmeg, and mix thoroughly. Taste and add salt and pepper if necessary.

Push a square of plastic film down into each greased ramekin.

Divide the fish mixture between the six lined ramekins, press it down with your fingers, and/or the back of a small spoon, and then smooth the tops with fingers or spoon. Fold the flaps of the plastic film over the top of the mixture. Refrigerate.

To serve as an amuse
If you are going to serve the mixture as an amuse, just put it all into a container and refrigerate. But using the six ramekins does give you the choice, to allow for a last-minute change of plan. Spoon small portions of the mixture into toast cups or onto toast disks, and garnish for example with slivers of black olives, or as desired.

To serve as an appetizer
Bring the filled ramekins nearly to room temperature before serving. If using orange slices as garnish, place an orange slice in the centre of each small plate. Unfold the top of the plastic wrapping, lift out the trout mixture in its cup of plastic film, and turn out onto the orange slice or directly on the plate.

If using the red pepper salad, put a spoonful on the plate. Then if using them, put half a tomato filled with horseradish mayonnaise on the plate, or do without the tomato cup and simply put a scoop of mayonnaise on the plate. Serve with toast fingers.

NOTES

Here, a small ramekin is about 75-millilitre capacity, 6.5 centimetres in diameter. For notes on lining a ramekin with plastic film, see Smoked Mackerel Spread.

Do not be tempted to use a sweet vermouth in this recipe. Of the dry vermouths, my clear preference is Noilly Prat.

Be careful when chopping up the fish. Wild fish are much more resistant to mashing, so there is little danger of making them too smooth, but farmed fish can go mushy very easily. Do not use a processor to chop the fish; this is one time you must use manual labour.

The slice of orange is entirely optional: its function is to make a decorative frame for the potted trout, so its diameter has to exceed that of the cylinder of trout. A medium orange (200 to 250 grams whole weight) works.

Tomato cups look nice on the plate. A medium-sized tomato works best—Campari for example. Cut in half around the equator (think of the stem end as the north pole), scoop out the seeds, and, if necessary, take a thin sliver off the end to help it sit upright on the plate.

For notes on making toast fingers or toast cups, see Salt Cod *Brandade*. For notes on making mayonnaise, see Salt Cod and Avocado Salad. For notes on roasting red peppers, see Hot-Smoked Salmon Pâté. For notes on vinaigrette, see Salt Cod and Potato Salad.

This soup is too substantial to be an appetizer at dinner, but it's perfect for a filling lunch.

TROUT CHOWDER

serves 4 to 6 as a lunch main course

200 g trout, trimmed weight
250 g leeks, trimmed weight
100 g celery, trimmed weight
3 garlic cloves
50 g butter
600 g potatoes, trimmed weight
750 ml trout stock
   (or fish or chicken stock)
1 tsp salt, or to taste
1/16 tsp cayenne
375 ml milk

Garnish
cream (optional)
chopped chives (optional)

Chop the leeks coarsely. Chop the celery finely. Mince the garlic finely. Cut the trimmed potatoes into 1- to 2-centimetre cubes. Trim the trout as per the Introductory Notes and cut into chunks similar to the potato.

Sweat the leeks, celery, and garlic in the butter until soft but not browned.

Add about 500 millilitres of the stock, the cubed potato, and the cayenne. Bring to a boil, then simmer until the potato is just soft.

Scoop out about 375 millilitres of this cooked mixture, add the remaining stock, and blend to a purée. Stir this back into the saucepan, add the milk, and bring back to barely a simmer. Add the cubed trout to the simmering soup, turn off the heat, and leave stand for 5 minutes to cook the fish.

Taste and add salt if needed. Add a few tablespoons of cream if liked (or add this to individual servings). Serve in warm soup plates or bowls, sprinkled with chives, and with crusty bread.

NOTES

The easiest way to chop leeks is to first cut the trimmed leeks lengthways into 4 to 6 long strips (depending on the size of the leek), then sliver crossways as thinly or thickly as you want. Similarly, for the celery stalks: cut them in halves or quarters lengthways according to size, then sliver thinly crossways.

Fish stock is usually never made with salmon or trout bones because they are too assertive for general use. But in this case the stock matches the principal ingredient and works harmoniously. If you have not made stock with the trout bones, use regular fish stock or chicken stock.

To blend part of the cooked mixture, transfer it to a tall, narrow jug that just fits your hand blender.

If you reheat this soup, bring it gently back to a simmer to avoid coagulating the milk. If it does become particulate, a little cream will mask it.

Well-buttered crusty bread is essential.

have loved this pairing ever since my mother first served me fried trout with bacon on the side when I was a small boy. This is an updated version.

TROUT with BACON

serves 4 as a main course

8 slices bacon
600 to 700 g trout, trimmed weight
4 tsp grainy mustard
salt and pepper
butter to grease a baking pan

Preheat the oven to 350°F. Trim the trout as per the Introductory Notes and cut into 4 portions about 150 to 175 grams each. If the trout fillets are thick, slice each portion in half horizontally. If fillets are thinner, make portions by stacking one piece on top of another.

Pre-cook the bacon: line a baking sheet with foil and turn up the rim. Put a wire cooling rack on top of the foil. Lay the bacon slices on the rack, perpendicular to the wires. Lay a second wire rack on top of the rashers. Bake about 30 to 35 minutes. Do not let the bacon totally get crisp—leave some flexibility. Reserve.

Grease a baking pan with butter. Lay one half of each portion of trout on the baking pan. If you have split a thicker piece of trout, lay the piece which originally had skin, skin-side down first. If you have clapped two thinner pieces together, lay either half skin-side down first.

Spread ½ teaspoon of the grainy mustard over each, and lay 2 cooked rashers on top—trim the ends of the bacon to leave them just protruding from the trout sandwich. Lay the other half of the split portion of trout, or the other thinner piece, on top. Spread another ½ teaspoon of mustard over the surface of each trout sandwich. Sprinkle lightly with salt and pepper.

Bake about 15 to 20 minutes or until just cooked.

Serve at once. Herbed fingerling potatoes and green beans are good accompaniments.

NOTES

This recipe works well with farmed trout.

Use the best bacon you can find: look for a dry-cure, thick-cut, commercial

bacon, or an artisanal bacon if you can find it. Turning up the rim of the foil is simply to catch the bacon fat and simplify cleanup.

Spread the mustard with a little spatula or small pastry brush.

For notes on testing for doneness with a small skewer, see Halibut Introductory Note, but in this case make sure you don't try to push the skewer through one of the rashers.

On the plate, this looks a bit like Potted Trout, but trout mousse is significantly different in both taste and texture. This recipe is much better with wild trout than farmed.

TROUT MOUSSE

makes 6 appetizers

350 g trout, trimmed weight
¾ tsp salt
½ tsp pepper
1 egg
1 egg white

Zest of ½ lemon
2 tbsp chives
125 ml cream
butter to grease muffin pan receptacles

Grease a six-receptacle, non-stick, standard muffin pan. Preheat the oven to 350°F. Have a kettle of boiling water on standby.

Trim the trout as per the Introductory Notes, cut into same-size chunks, and transfer to a food processor with the salt, pepper, egg, and egg white. Process until very smooth, scraping down the processor bowl a few times to make sure all lumps of fish are pulverized before the cream goes in. Add the zest and chives, and pulse. Add the cream and pulse a few times just to mix.

Divide this mixture between the six greased receptacles, smoothing the top of each with the back of a small spoon.

Bake in a *bain-marie* for about 25 minutes or until the mousses are just firm to the touch. Remove from the oven, run a sharp toothpick around the rim of each mousse where it may be baked onto the pan, and turn the mousses out onto a rack to cool. When cool, wrap each in plastic film, and refrigerate.

To serve, unwrap each mousse and put on a small, chilled plate. Garnish the plate with salad of your choice; try a mixture of cherry tomatoes and roasted red peppers with this mousse. Crusty bread is a necessary complement.

NOTES

A standard-size muffin pan has 6, 8, or 12 receptacles, each about 7 centimetres in diameter across the top, and 3 centimetres deep.

It helps to stabilize the fish purée if everything is kept very cold during its preparation. It is important to make sure the fish is completely puréed before you add the cream. Make sure to scrape down the sides of the processor frequently and check the fish very carefully for lumps before adding other ingredients. Then, do not run the food processor continuously after adding the cream—you risk making it into butter; just pulse intermittently to mix it in.

For the *bain-marie,* find a rectangular dish that will hold the muffin pan comfortably. For notes on using a *bain-marie,* see the comments under Smoked Cod Custards.

I f you don't have enough precious wild-caught trout for the previous recipe, remember that fish mousses are versatile things in the kitchen and small amounts of trout—or other tasty fish or shellfish—can be made into flavourful dishes by wrapping the mousse in sole fillets, for instance. This is an example of what the French call *paupiettes*: thin slices of meat, fowl, or fish wrapped around a savoury filling.

TROUT MOUSSE WRAPPED in SOLE

serves 4 as a main course

400 g sole

Trout mousse
175 g trout, trimmed weight
1 egg
⅜ tsp salt
6 tbsp cream

Poaching stock
375 ml fish stock
125 ml white wine
50 g shallot, trimmed weight
50 g celery, trimmed weight
50 g carrot, trimmed weight
2 allspice berries, whole
½ garlic clove

Sauce
2 tbsp flour
50 g butter
¼ teaspoon salt
2 to 3 tablespoons cream, or to taste
1 red pepper
milk if needed to thin the sauce

Garnish
parsley (optional)

Trout mousse
Trim the trout as per the Introductory Notes, cut into same-size pieces, transfer to a food processor with the egg and salt, and process until smooth. Then add the cream and pulse to mix. Reserve in the refrigerator.

Poaching stock
Chop the shallot, celery, carrot, and garlic. Put these and all the other poaching stock ingredients in a small saucepan, bring to a boil, and simmer about 30 minutes. Strain, and press down on the solids to extract all the fluid. Discard the solids, reserve the strained fluid.

Sole rolls
If necessary, trim the sole fillets, removing any skin or bone. Lay each fillet skin-side

up on a work surface. Spread about 2 table-spoons of trout mousse along each fillet, then roll up, starting at thick end. Secure the roll with a toothpick.

Bring the reserved poaching fluid to a simmer, gently slide in the sole rolls, then cover and cook on the lowest possible heat about 10 minutes. If using immediately, keep warm; if to be used later, refrigerate. Strain the poaching liquid, discard any remaining solids, put the fluid back in the saucepan, and simmer until reduced to about 250 millilitres.

Sauce
Roast the red pepper, remove the charred skin, core, and seeds. Sliver the roasted flesh into strips as thin as possible. Reserve.

Melt the 50 grams of butter in a small saucepan, stir in the flour and cook on very low heat about 5 minutes. Whisk in the reserved, reduced poaching fluid and bring back to a boil. Reduce the heat and simmer about 5 minutes. Add cream to taste and adjust the seasoning. Thin the sauce with a little stock or milk if liked.

To serve
Reheat the sauce, reheat the sole rolls in the warm sauce. Gently stir in the reserved roasted red pepper. Transfer it all to a warmed serving dish. Garnish with minced parsley. Or make individual servings: lay two warm sole rolls in each of four warmed soup plates and divide the sauce between the four. Gently stir in about one-quarter of the roasted red pepper slivers into each bowl. Garnish with minced parsley.

NOTES

See the notes in the previous recipe about keeping ingredients cold while making the mousse and not over-processing the cream.

Use one or two (or more) toothpicks to secure each sole roll as required. The best toothpicks are bamboo.

For notes on roasting red peppers, see Hot-Smoked Salmon Pâté.

*Trout Mousse
Wrapped in Sole*

This is a complete meal cooked in one package. What goes in the package with the fish is flexible, so feel free to change any of the suggestions below to suit yourself. But as a guideline I think it's good to have a starchy component on the bottom—potato, sweet potato, rice, polenta—and an interesting but complementary mixture of vegetables on top. Don't be afraid to experiment: it's difficult to go too far wrong, as long as you remember that any vegetables will need pre-cooking because they will not soften in the time it takes the fish to cook.

This is less tedious than it looks, and because all the preparation is done in advance it makes an ideal dinner with guests where you don't want to be at the stove dealing with a lot of last-minute details.

TROUT WRAPPED in PARCHMENT

serves 4 as a main course

600 to 700 g trout, trimmed weight
100 g bacon
4 tbsp water
butter as needed

Suggested accompaniments
200 g leeks
100 g mushrooms
2 garlic cloves
4 tbsp white wine
12 grape tomatoes, or 2 red peppers
300 g sweet potatoes, trimmed weight
either 32 to 40 green beans,
    or 16 to 20 sugar peas
salt and pepper to taste

Sliver the leek into thin half moons. Slice the whole mushrooms, or cut them in half first if large. Finely chop the garlic. Cut the bacon into 5-millimetre cubes.

If using tomatoes, remove the skins (optional). If using red peppers, roast, trim, and sliver thinly. Cut the peeled sweet potatoes into 1-centimetre-thick rounds and poach in boiling salted water until tender (6 or 7 minutes), then drain and reserve. Poach the green beans or sugar peas in boiling salted water until tender (time will vary with the nature of the bean or pea) then plunge into cold water; drain and reserve.

Cut four squares of parchment paper, about 30 by 30 centimetres. Cut four squares of foil, about 35 by 35 centimetres. Trim the trout as per the Introductory Notes and divide into four portions, about 150 to 175 grams each. Preheat the oven to 350°F.

Sweat the bacon with the water on low heat until some fat is liberated. Then raise the heat slightly to fry the bacon in its own fat. Fry until a lot of fat has rendered, but do not crisp the bacon bits. Remove and reserve them. If necessary, add a little butter to bacon fat left in the pan to make up about 2 tablespoons. Or if there is an excess of bacon fat, discard all but 2 tablespoons.

Sweat the leeks, mushrooms, and garlic in the remaining bacon fat/butter. When soft and the mushrooms have released their flu-id, add the wine and evaporate to a glaze. Mix with the cooked bacon and reserve.

Lay the parchment squares on a work surface. Place one-quarter of the sweet potato rounds in the centre of each in one layer but packed tightly together. Spread one-quarter of the leek-mushroom-bacon mixture on top. Lay a portion of trout on top of this. Arrange six skinned tomato halves—or one-quarter of the slivered roasted red pepper—on top of the trout, and one-quarter of the beans or peas on top of them. Fold up the sides and ends of the parchment. Then wrap these in foil, crimping the edges to seal as tightly as possible. Place on a baking sheet and bake 30 minutes.

To serve, remove the foil, and lay the food in its parchment on a warmed shallow bowl.

NOTES

For notes on peeling tomatoes, see Halibut in Spicy Coconut Sauce. Cut the peeled tomatoes in half. But if peeling is a step too far for you, leave the skins on.

For notes on roasting red peppers, see Hot-Smoked Salmon Pâté.

Salted water is 1 teaspoon of salt per litre of water. Test the disks of sweet potato frequently with a small skewer after they have simmered about 5 minutes because they will easily overcook.

Wrap the food in parchment as if wrapping a parcel: bring two sides up and over the food to overlap on top. Then flatten the parchment at the free ends, fold the sides diagonally over each other, and fold the points over the top of the package. It helps to put a small plate on top of each wrapped package to stop it unfolding itself while you attend to the others. Fold the foil to seal the package more tightly: crimp together the edges of the first fold to make a tight seal, then repeatedly fold over the other ends to seal tightly.

I like to serve this with foil removed but each portion still in its parchment wrapper: remove the foil, place the parchment parcel on a warmed, shallow soup dish, and fold back the corners of the parchment to attractively display the food. A slightly more informal approach is to simply place the complete package—complete with foil—on the plate and let each guest peel back the wrappings as they please. But if you prefer to present the food completely unwrapped, remove the foil from each as they come out of the oven and slide the contents of each package directly onto a warmed dish.

Chapter Nine

TURBOT

Reinhardtius hippoglossoides

SALT TURBOT

Salt Turbot Soup

Salt Turbot Cakes

SMOKED TURBOT

Smoked Turbot Kedgeree

Smoked Turbot Hot Smokies

Smoked Turbot Omelette

Do not confuse the highly esteemed—and therefore highly expensive—eastern Atlantic turbot with the fish called turbot on the western side of the Atlantic. They are two completely different species; both are flatfish, but that's the only thing they have in common.

The eastern Atlantic is home to the European turbot, *Scophthalmus maximus*, a sinistral flatfish (eyes on the left side of the head), and when European cookbooks talk of turbot this is what they mean. On the western side of the Atlantic we have a dextral (eyes right) species, which does in fact occur in the colder parts of the eastern Atlantic, but is completely overshadowed commercially by the European turbot.

Our western turbot is also called Greenland halibut, or Greenland turbot, or simply turbot in Newfoundland and other places on the eastern seaboard of North America.

Fresh turbot is a tasty fish, excellent simply baked or fried in butter or ghee. But it truly excels when it has been salted or smoked.

INTRODUCTORY NOTES ON SALT AND SMOKED TURBOT

Salt turbot was much loved in the traditional Newfoundland kitchen and preferred to fresh turbot by many. Typically, it was served simply soaked and poached, sometimes with drawn butter or egg sauce.

The yield from salt turbot is about 40 to 50 per cent of the untrimmed, on-the-bone, salted weight—so start with about 1 kilogram whole, salted weight if you need about 400 to 500 grams cooked, trimmed weight. If in doubt, underestimate the yield, because a bit of extra fish can always be absorbed by the recipe.

Salt turbot seems more reluctant than salt cod to lose its salt when soaked, so I soak it at least 48 hours, with several changes of water, or 72 hours for thicker pieces.

Choose a wide saucepan (with a lid) that will hold your salt turbot comfortably—cut the fish, if necessary, to make it fit. Bring 3 or 4 litres of water to the boil in this, slide in the soaked, salt turbot, put on the lid, turn off the heat, and leave the fish cook for 5 or 10 minutes according to thickness. Lift the fish out of the water, and when cool enough to handle, pick the meat off the bones, trying to keep the big blocks of meat intact—although if fish cakes are your plan it doesn't really matter.

Smoked turbot will usually be bought as smoked fillets, with or without the skin. So the weight you buy is pretty much the finished weight, although you may have to remove the skin after cooking the fish.

SALT TURBOT

With its emphasis on garlic, and the addition of a pungent rust-coloured (hence the French name *rouille*), peppery mayonnaise, this approximates to a *bourride*, but I have not called it that because the purists will insist that it is not "real" *bourride*.

This is not a soup to serve as an appetizer at dinner—try it for lunch.

SALT TURBOT SOUP

serves 4 as a main course lunch

**200 to 250 g salt turbot, soaked,
  cooked, trimmed weight**
150 g onion, trimmed weight
200 g fennel bulb, trimmed weight
150 g leek, trimmed weight
3 garlic cloves
25 g butter
2 strips orange zest
**750 ml stock, equal parts fish
  and vegetable**
1 bay leaf
½ batch rouille mayonnaise

Garnish
chopped fennel fronds (optional)

Soak and cook the salt turbot as per the Introductory Notes and keep the meat warm. Dice the onion, fennel, and leek into 1-centimetre pieces. Mince the garlic. Finely chop the fennel fronds.

Sweat the onion, fennel (but not the fronds), leek, and garlic in the butter until soft. Add the orange zest, bay leaf, and stock. Bring to a boil and simmer about 20 minutes. Then remove the bay leaf and zest, blend all or part of the rest of the mixture. Refrigerate if to be used later.

Bring the soup back to a simmer, turn off the heat and stir in about half the rouille mayonnaise. Divide this between four warmed soup dishes. Sprinkle each dish with chopped fennel fronds.

Lay a portion of cooked fish—about 50 to 75 grams—on top of the garnished soup, and put 1 tablespoon of rouille mayonnaise on top of each piece of fish.

NOTES

For this recipe soak the salt turbot for at least 72 hours because this soup needs less residual saltiness than the turbot cakes of the next recipe. If you

are sensitive to salt, then soak the salt turbot for even longer, keeping it refrigerated while doing so.

For the orange zest, take two broad strips off a small (150 grams) orange with a vegetable peeler.

How much of the soup to blend is a matter of personal preference. Sometimes I blend it all to a smooth slurry. Sometimes I stick my hand blender into the saucepan and just give it a few pulses. Sometimes I scoop out a portion of the soup and blend it completely in a separate jug and then return it to the saucepan. It's very much a matter of the mood of the moment.

If the fronds of the fennel are damaged, or mouldy, or had been stripped off before you bought it, use chopped parsley as a garnish.

For notes on making rouille mayonnaise, see Salt Cod and Avocado Salad. This is a pungent, spicy sauce, so reduce (or increase) the amounts of garlic and cayenne to your taste. The paprika is just for colour—although it can be tasted in the sauce—and an equally rusty colour can be achieved by adding pureed, roasted red pepper, and/or a pinch or two of soaked saffron. Both of these will also subtly change the taste of the sauce.

A book about fish without fish cakes (other than the *brandade* fish cakes already mentioned) is unthinkable. Cooks make fish cakes from all manner of fish, both fresh and salted, and because they are so popular there is an inevitable and perpetual debate about which is the best. That debate will of course never be resolved—but for *my* personal taste the absolute apotheosis of the fish cake is one made with salt fish, either salt cod or salt turbot.

SALT TURBOT CAKES

serves 4 to 6 as a main course

500 g salt turbot, soaked,
  cooked, trimmed weight
500 g potatoes, trimmed weight
  (or same weight as the cooked turbot)
250 g shallots, trimmed weight
  (or half the weight of the cooked turbot)
30 g butter
50 g ghee for frying
1 tsp pepper
flour for dusting

Soak and cook the salt turbot as per the Introductory Notes. Slice the shallots thinly into half moons, then sweat in the butter until completely soft but not browned.

Cook the potatoes in salted water until completely tender, then drain and reserve.

Mash the cooked turbot coarsely. Mix in the cooked shallots, pepper, and potato. Stir them together, but do not mash to a purée: leave the texture coarse.

Divide this mixture into 8 or 12 portions (about 100 or 150 g respectively) and press each into a little cake about 2.5 to 3 centimetres thick.

Heat a frying pan on medium-high heat and put in a portion of the ghee. Dust each fish cake with flour, lay two or three in the hot pan, and fry 2 to 4 minutes on each side until well browned on both sides. Reserve these in a warm place while you fry the remaining fish cakes.

NOTES

This is equally good—some would say better—when made from salt cod.

See the Introductory Notes about calculating the yield of cooked salt turbot. And if you end up with more than you expected, just make each turbot cake fractionally larger.

I prefer to use a yellow-fleshed potato for fish cakes, but a high-starch potato like a russet can be used with success. If you use the latter, cook them
in their skins to avoid them falling apart when boiled. Leave them until
cool enough to handle, then peel and use the same weight as the cooked
turbot.

See the notes about ghee under Salt Cod *Brandade* Fish Cakes.

SMOKED TURBOT

Smoked turbot is only becoming popular in Newfoundland and Labrador now that local, high-quality, artisanally smoked turbot is more available. No less an authority than Alan Davidson in his definitive book *North Atlantic Seafood* considers smoking the best treatment for our turbot (which he calls Greenland Halibut). I totally agree, and our locally smoked turbot is the best I have had anywhere. Here are four recipes which will help introduce this not-very-well-known Newfoundland product to a wider audience.

The origin of modern kedgeree is the Indian *khichri*, a dish of lentils, rice, and spices. This was adopted, adapted, and transformed in the kitchens of the British Raj into the modern dish of fish (usually smoked), rice, and spices. It is still a popular British breakfast dish, usually made with smoked haddock, but I think our smoked turbot makes an even better dish.

SMOKED TURBOT KEDGEREE

serves 4 to 6 as a main course

350 g smoked turbot, raw weight
250 g basmati rice
200 g onion
50 g butter
1½ tsp kedgeree spices (below)
½ tsp salt
375 ml chicken stock

Spice mixture
Equal parts by volume of cumin, coriander, and turmeric, with ½ part cayenne

Garnishes (optional)
250 g onion
1 tsp oil
2 to 4 eggs
paprika
parsley

Wash and soak the rice. Chop the 200 grams of onion into 1-centimetre dice. Slice the raw, smoked turbot thinly after removing any skin. Hard boil the eggs if using them.

Slice the 250 grams of onion into thick quarter-circles.

Sweat the 200 grams of chopped onion in the butter on low heat until soft and translucent but not browned (about 20 to 30 minutes). Add the spices and cook another 2 to 3 minutes.

Drain the soaked rice, stir into the cooked 200 grams of onion and spices and cook on low heat until all the residual water on the rice has evaporated and the rice is starting to stick to the saucepan. Add the chicken stock and salt. Bring to a boil, then simmer briefly on medium heat until the fluid is partly absorbed, and small, bubbling craters appear on the surface of the rice, about 2 or 3 minutes.

Now quickly add the sliced fish, spreading it out over the surface of the rice, put the lid on the saucepan, turn the heat down as low as possible, and cook for about 20 minutes. Turn off the heat and leave sit with the lid on until ready to serve.

Garnishes (optional)
Fry the 250 grams of sliced onion in the oil until lightly browned. Hard boil the eggs. Finely chop the parsley.

To serve
Cut the hard-boiled eggs into halves or quarters lengthways. Mix the cooked fish into the rice it's sitting on, then spread this mixture in a serving dish. Spread the fried onions evenly over the surface, and arrange the pieces of egg on top. If liked, dust paprika over each egg, and sprinkle a little chopped parsley over the lot.

NOTES

Rice should usually be washed and soaked before use; see the notes under Cod Biryani.

Although I list the garnishes as optional, personally I never make this without the fried onions and hard-boiled eggs—they both complement this dish.

If you don't have your own way of hard boiling eggs, see the notes on hard-boiled eggs under Salt Cod, Potato, and Onion Casserole.

"Fry the 250 grams of sliced onion in the oil until lightly browned" is a deceptively simple instruction, because onions can be fried in so many different ways. For this recipe I think they should be browned and lightly caramelized: see the notes under Salt Cod, Potato, and Onion Casserole.

These make an interesting appetizer, or a main-course lunch if served with salad and crusty bread.

SMOKED TURBOT HOT SMOKIES

serves 6 as a light lunch or as an appetizer

200 g smoked turbot, raw weight
300 g tomatoes, peeled, trimmed weight
2 tbsp butter
2 tbsp flour
250 ml milk
¼ tsp salt, or to taste
¼ tsp pepper, or to taste
¼ tsp nutmeg, or to taste

Peel, core, and deseed the tomatoes. Chop them into 0.5-centimetre pieces and leave to drain in a sieve. Cut the raw turbot into 1- to 2-centimetre pieces, after removing any skin.

Make a béchamel sauce from the butter, flour, and milk. Preheat the oven to 425°F.

Mix the drained, chopped tomatoes, chopped turbot, salt, pepper, and nutmeg. Then mix with the béchamel. Taste and add more salt, pepper, and nutmeg as needed.

Divide between six ramekins. Smooth the tops of the mixture with the back of a small spoon.

Bake about 30 minutes.

NOTES

Any flavourful fresh tomato works here. For notes on peeling tomatoes, see Halibut in Spicy Coconut Curry Sauce, but here remove the seeds as well: cut tomatoes in two around the equator (stem end is north pole), hold a half tomato in the palm of your hand and squeeze gently while pushing out the bulk of the seeds with your thumb from the seed-pockets. But don't get fussy: you don't have to remove absolutely every seed.

To get the 300 grams trimmed weight of tomatoes, I start with about 450 grams of whole, untrimmed Campari tomatoes.

For notes on béchamel sauce, see Cod Hot Pot.

I use standard ramekins for this recipe: about 150-millilitre capacity, 7.5 by 3.5 centimetres diameter by depth.

This can also be made by using cream rather than a béchamel sauce: divide the fish-tomato-salt-spices mixture between the ramekins, and pour enough cream into each to almost cover the mixture. The result tends to be a bit messier because the cream bubbles over the edge, but tastes excellent.

This is equally good made with smoked cod.

This is very much in the style of Omelette Arnold Bennett, invented for Bennett by chefs at the Savoy in London when he was staying there while writing his two novels set in that hotel—or some say when he dined there after the theatre when he was working as a drama critic.

Some of the original versions are quite complex, involving Hollandaise sauce to further enrich an already rich dish. You can still see it on menus in British restaurants, often considerably simplified, as mine is. But the essential synergy of smoked fish and eggs has been retained.

SMOKED TURBOT OMELETTE

serves 2 as a lunch or brunch main course

150 g smoked turbot, raw weight
125 ml milk
125 ml cream
1 shallot
1 clove
1 bay leaf
6 eggs
20 g parmesan
2 pinches salt
2 pinches pepper
4 tbsp chives
15 g butter

Thinly slice the shallot. Grate the parmesan. Chop the chives. Cut the raw smoked turbot into pieces that will fit in one layer in the saucepan you are going to use; if there is any skin, leave it on for now. Preheat the broiler.

Put the milk, cream, sliced shallot, clove, and bay leaf in the saucepan. Bring to a simmer, then turn off the heat and leave to infuse about 30 minutes.

Put the pieces of raw smoked turbot into the milk-cream mixture in the saucepan, bring back to a simmer, cover the saucepan, turn off the heat, and let the fish poach for about 5 minutes or until it flakes easily when prodded. Lift the fish from the saucepan, trim off any skin, flake the trimmed flesh coarsely, and reserve.

Pass the milk-cream poaching fluid through a fine strainer, pressing down hard on the cooked shallot to extract as much fluid as possible. Discard the solids, return the strained fluid to the saucepan, and simmer on low heat until reduced to about 125 millilitres. Set aside to cool. When cool, whisk in the grated parmesan.

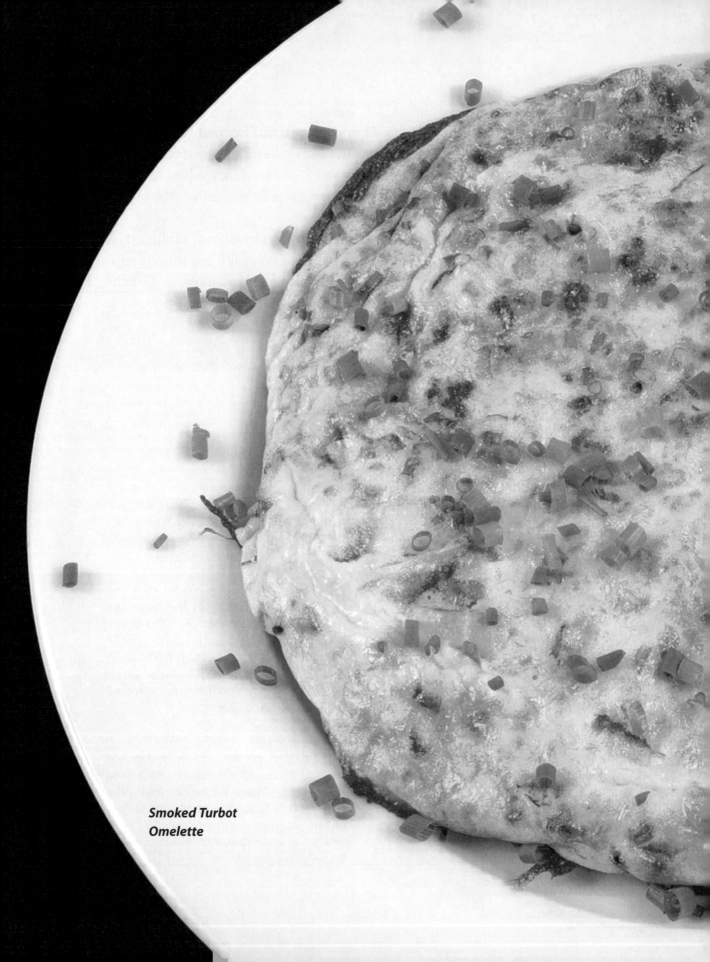

Smoked Turbot Omelette

Whisk three of the eggs together with a pinch of salt and pepper. Whisk in half the reduced cream-parmesan mixture. Stir in half the cooked, smoked turbot and 1 tablespoon of chopped chives.

Heat a 20-centimetre crepe or omelette pan over medium heat. When hot, put in half the butter and swirl to coat the pan.

Scrape the three-egg mixture into the hot, buttered pan, and as it starts to set around the edges, immediately start pulling the mixture in from the edges toward the centre, tipping the pan as you do so to make the liquid part in the middle flow into the space you have created. When the mixture is part-cooked but still liquid in the middle, put the whole pan under the hot broiler. Move it around to brown the top evenly—about 2 or 3 minutes total, or until the mixture is patched with brown but still squidgy in the middle.

Turn out onto a warm plate and sprinkle with a tablespoon of chopped chives. Reserve this in a warm place while you whisk the other three eggs and repeat the process to make a second omelette.

NOTES

The finished omelettes should be soft in the middle, what the French call *baveuse*, often simply defined as runny, but which in the kitchen has a more precise meaning: neither fluid nor completely firm, but just in that middle zone of semi-set.

This recipe scales up—or down—to make omelettes for 1 to 6 people; but there are considerations. An omelette for one is tricky because reducing only a half cup of milk-cream risks drying it out completely, or leaving most of it dried on the sides of the pan. But it can be done with care. On the other hand, with larger numbers, the reduction is easier, but the problem is to keep the first few warm without overcooking while you cook the rest. I find the ideal number to cook this for is two, three, or four.

BIBLIOGRAPHY

Principally authors and books mentioned in the text, together with some that readers might consult to both enlarge their fish-cooking repertoire and their knowledge of fish in general.

Brown, Dale, ed. *The Cooking of Scandinavia*. Foods of the World Series. New York: Time-Life Books, 1968.

Collingham, Lizzie. *The Hungry Empire: How Britain's Quest for Food Shaped the Modern World*. London: The Bodley Head, 2017.

Courtine, Robert, ed. *Larousse Gastronomique*. Paris: Libraire Larousse, 1984. English ed., 1988 by Hamlyn Publishing.

Davidson, Alan. *North Atlantic Seafood*. New York: Viking Press, 1979.

Davidson, Alan. *The Oxford Companion to Food*. Oxford: Oxford University Press, 1999.

Grigson, Jane. *Fish Cookery*. Exeter, England: David and Charles, 1973.

Jones, Edward A. *Salt Cod Cuisine*. Portugal Cove-St. Philip's, NL: Boulder Publications, 2013.

Pickavance, Roger. *The Traditional Newfoundland Kitchen*. Portugal Cove-St. Philip's, NL: Boulder Publications, 2017.

Pickavance, Roger. *From Rum to Rhubarb: Modern Recipes for Newfoundland Fruits, vegetables, and berries*. Portugal Cove-St. Philip's, NL: Boulder Books, 2019.

Smith, Andrew F., ed. *The Oxford Encyclopedia of Food and Drink in America*. 2nd ed. Oxford: Oxford University Press, 2013.

I want to thank the crew of Boulder Books—particularly Gavin, Amanda, Stephanie, Iona, and Todd—for their forbearance, expertise, and skill.

Roger Pickavance was raised in the Welsh Borders, where his lifelong interest in food and cooking started with fruit and vegetables from his parents' garden, trout from local rivers, and Welsh lamb from the hills behind his home. His memories of those tastes are still the benchmarks by which he judges food today. His father was a keen ornithologist, his mother knowledgeable about wild flowers. Their love of the natural world started Roger on the path to a PhD in biology, which in turn led to a faculty position at Memorial University. Now retired, Roger lives, cooks, and writes in St. John's. His first three cookbooks, *From Rum to Rhubarb, The Traditional Newfoundland Kitchen* (2017) and *Agnes Ayre's Notebook* (2018), were published by Boulder Books.